D1029756

Reed Instruments

The Montagu Collection: An Annotated Catalogue

Jeremy Montagu

Fallen Leaf Reference Books in Music, No. 36

The Scarecrow Press, Inc.
Lanham, Maryland, and London
2001

SCARECROW PRESS, INC.

Published in the United States of America
by Scarecrow Press, Inc.
4720 Boston Way, Lanham, Maryland 20706
www.scarecrowpress.com

4 Pleydell Gardens, Folkestone
Kent CT20 2DN, England

British Library Cataloguing-in-Publication Information Available

Library of Congress Cataloging-in-Publication Data

Montagu, Jeremy.
    The Montagu collection : an annotated catalogue / [Jeremy Montagu].
      p. cm.—(Fallen Leaf reference books in music, ISSN 8755-268X ; 36)
    Includes bibliographical references and index.
    Contents:—v. 4, pt. 2. Reed instruments.
    ISBN 0-8108-3938-5 (alk. paper)
    1. Musical instruments—Catalog and collections. 2. Montagu, Jeremy—Musical
instrument collections—Catalogs. I. Title. II. Fallen Leaf reference books in music ;
no. 36

ML462.O95 M66 2001
784.19'074—dc21 98-54472

♾️ TM   The paper used in this publication meets the minimum requirements of
American National Statndard for Information Sciences—Permanence of
Paper for Printed Library Materials, ANSI/NISO Z39.48-1992.
Manufactured in the United States of America.

In gratitude to
Dr. Otto Samson,
sometime curator of the Horniman Museum, London,
who first introduced me to the fascination
of the instruments of other musics.

May his memory be for a blessing.

Contents

List of Illustrations

Forked Shawm

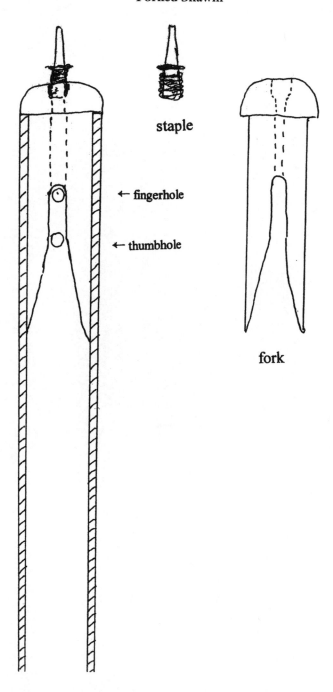

staple

← fingerhole

← thumbhole

fork

11+ key Oboe
drawn by Testu Ito

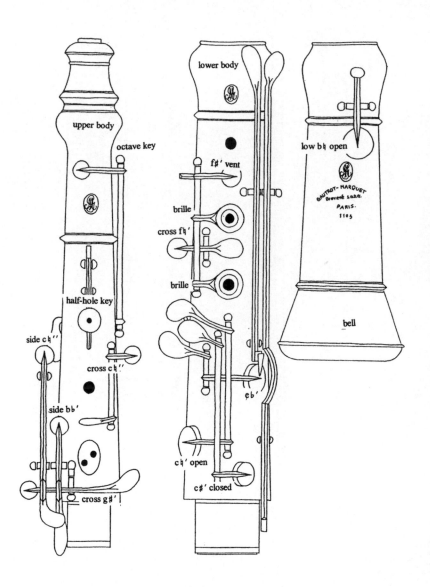

Thumb-Plate System
Oboe, X 4
drawn by Testu Ito

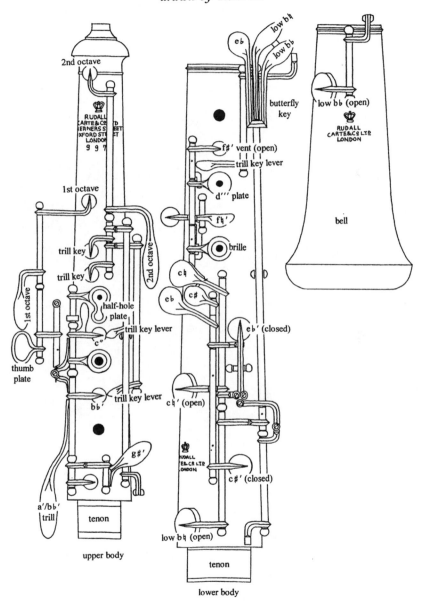

- 2nd octave
- RUDALL CARTE&C? LTD BERNERS STREET OXFORD STREET LONDON 997
- 1st octave
- trill key
- trill key
- 1st octave
- half-hole plate
- trill key lever
- c''
- thumb plate
- trill key lever
- bb'
- 2nd octave
- g#'
- a'/bb' trill
- tenon
- upper body

- eb
- low b♮
- low bb
- butterfly key
- f#' vent (open)
- trill key lever
- d''' plate
- f♮'
- brille
- c♮
- c#
- eb
- eb' (closed)
- c♮' (open)
- RUDALL CARTE&C? LTD LONDON
- c#' (closed)
- low b♮ (open)
- tenon
- lower body

- low b♮
- low bb (open)
- RUDALL CARTE&C? LTD LONDON
- bell

French-system Bassoon

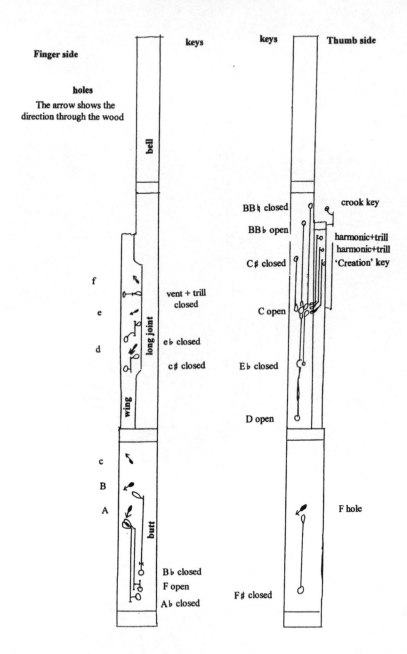

German-system Bassoon

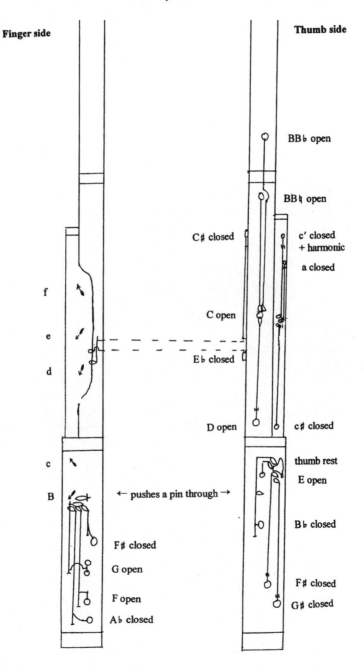

6 key Clarinet

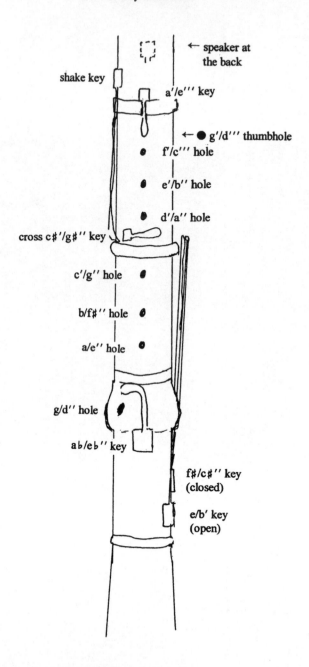

← speaker at the back

shake key

a'/e''' key

← ● g'/d''' thumbhole

f'/c''' hole

e'/b'' hole

d'/a'' hole

cross c♯'/g♯'' key

c'/g'' hole

b/f♯'' hole

a/e'' hole

g/d'' hole

a♭/e♭'' key

f♯/c♯'' key
(closed)

e/b' key
(open)

13+ key Clarinet

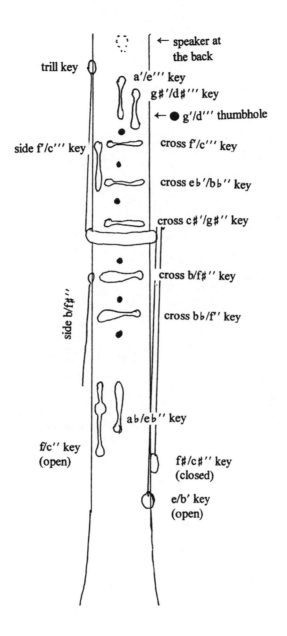

← speaker at the back

trill key

a'/e''' key

g#'/d#''' key

← ● g'/d''' thumbhole

side f'/c''' key

cross f'/c''' key

cross eb'/bb'' key

cross c#'/g#'' key

cross b/f#'' key

side b/f#''

cross bb/f' key

ab/eb'' key

f/c'' key
(open)

f#/c#'' key
(closed)

e/b' key
(open)

Idioglot/Heterozeug
Single Reeds

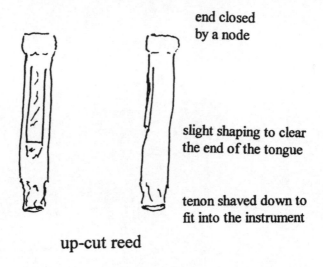

end closed
by a node

slight shaping to clear
the end of the tongue

tenon shaved down to
fit into the instrument

up-cut reed

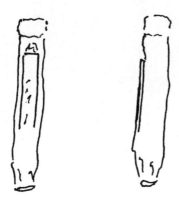

down-cut reed

Preface

This is the first of a series of descriptive and annotated catalogues, all of which are arranged more or less in the order established by Eric Moritz von Hornbostel and Curt Sachs in 1914. Thus volume 4 covers the aerophones or wind instruments, and part 2 thereof the reed instruments. In due course it will be followed by parts 1 (flutes and whistles) and 3 (trumpets and horns) and volumes 1, 2, and 3 for the other classes of idiophones, membranophones, and chordophones.

This collection, of worldwide coverage and all types of instruments, began to take shape in the early 1960s when what had been a small and very random collection, mainly of professional percussion kit (which covers a wide range of instrument types, for drummers play all the odds and ends which other musicians deem to be beneath their dignity) was then rapidly expanded to illustrate lectures, and to provide material for research, on all aspects of organology. By 1967, when I mounted an exhibition in Sheffield and for that reason started my ledger catalogue, the number of instruments had reached about 450. It has now, thirty-five years later, reached nearly 2,500. It is always accessible to interested persons, but only by appointment for the simple reason that I need to be there to open the door.

Jeremy Montagu

Abbreviations

O = overall
L = length
W = width
Th = thickness [th is also used to indicate thumbhole]
ø = diameter

All dimensions are given from the end nearest the player's mouth, always referred to as the upper end even when, for example compared with a bassoon's long joint or bell, it is actually nearer the ground. Following the example of Phillip T. Young in his recent catalogue of the Linz collection, the measurements of all instruments made in separate joints are taken excluding any tenons; these are then shown as (+zz) before the main measurement, if at the upper end, and after it if at the other end. Equally, the depth of all sockets is given as (-yy) and similarly placed. Fingerhole measurements are given from the upper end, the thumbhole (th) coming according to its position relative to the fingerholes. A double slash // shows the division between one joint and the next. Where fingerholes are oval, the first measurement is along the bore and the second across it. All measurements are in millimetres.

φ = photograph and/or slide, followed by the number of the negative;
b/w = black and white
col sl = colour slide
c. = *circa*, about

int = internal
ext = external

As usual, in transcriptions of makers' or other marks, a single slash /
denotes a new line, and a double slash and spacer /# / denotes a larger gap
or different location on the instrument. Words in [square brackets] describe
iconographic or other non-verbal elements in such marks.

CUMAE = Cambridge University Museum of Archæology & Ethnography.

FoMRHIQ = *Fellowship of Makers & Researchers of Historical Instruments Quarterly.*

GSJ = *Galpin Society Journal.*

JAMIS = *Journal of the American Musical Instrument Society.*

LERP = Laurence Picken, *Folk Musical Instruments of Turkey.*

NLI = William Waterhouse, *The New Langwill Index.*

PTY = Phillip T. Young, *4900 Historical Woodwind Instruments.*

JM Scales = Jeremy Montagu, *The Scales of Music*, a special exhibition catalogue for the British Association for Science Set7, March 1994, Bate Collection, Oxford.

My original catalogue is in ledgers, so that catalogue numbers are
those of the volume in Roman numbers (I-XII so far), the page in Arabic
numbers, and, where there is more than one instrument on a page, a letter.

Sources of acquisitions, unless otherwise specified, are usually London,
but some, especially from the earlier days of the collection, were not
recorded and are now forgotten. Such few dates as are known are noted.
Because the ledger catalogue was begun in order to establish what I had, so
as to decide what to include in the 1967 Sheffield Exhibition, all instruments numbered lower than III 170 must have been acquired before that
year.

Reed Instruments

Jeremy Montagu

Part I
Double Reeds

AEROPHONES—4

The definition in the Hornbostel & Sachs *Systematik* is "The air itself is the vibrator in the primary sense." With the exception of the flutes this is simply not true; the primary vibrator is one or more idiophonic lamellae, commonly known as reeds, or, in the case of the "brass" the player's lips ("brass" is a convenient short term for all lip-vibrated aerophones whether, like the orchestral and brass band instruments, they are made of brass or not). If one looks behind what makes the reeds or lips vibrate, then indeed the answer is air, but in that case, the "primary vibrator" for chordophones is a plectrum, fingers, or bow, for idiophones hands or beaters, and so forth. If by "primary vibrator" is meant "what generates the sound" (for idiophones the body of the instrument, for drums a membrane, and for chordophones a string), then the answer here is air for the flutes, reeds for the reed instruments, and lips (a special form of retreating reed) for the brass. Admittedly, what establishes the pitch for the instruments classified under 42 (wind instruments proper) is the length, shape, and vibratory mode of the coupled air column, and thus the air has a greater importance for those instruments but this is specifically excluded for all those instruments in 41: *Free aerophones. The vibrating air is not confined by the instrument.* As a result, I find this whole section of the *Systematik* very difficult to deal with in this respect.

Certainly a vibrating column of air turns the squawk of a reed or the lips into musical sound, but the basic principle of all other sections of the *Systematik* is that classification depends on what generates the sound; thus a violin is a chordophone because the sound is generated by the vibration of the strings, and not an idiophone nor an aerophone, even though the sound of the strings alone would be all but inaudible, and therefore the sound that we hear must be amplified by the wood of the belly and by the air contained within the box. Here, however, that principle is abandoned and we have a separate section for the *Free Aerophones*, and another, 422, *Reedpipes*, for all the instruments whose sound is generated by the reeds already subsumed under 412.1, *Idiophonic Interruptive Aerophones or Reeds.* This is not a logical procedure, and indeed it was precisely this illogicality which started John Burton and me on the search for a better method. Partly because of the difficulties encountered in using our system, partly because we are better off with a system which people will use internationally, however illogical it may be, than with a system that they won't use, but chiefly because of Laurence Picken's remarks in his essay on classification in his *Folk Musical Instruments of Turkey*, 558 ff (henceforth *LERP*), I have reverted, with and subject to the comments scattered throughout this catalogue, to the Hornbostel & Sachs *Systematik*. Not, please note, to the development of it which was evolved by our French colleagues in CIMCIM, which had all the faults of the Hornbostel & Sachs, plus a great many new ones of its own.

However, in the arrangement of this catalogue I have taken the liberty of dividing those instruments which should come together under 412 into their types, taking the concussion reeds (412.11) with the double-reed instruments (422.1), the percussion reeds (412.12) with the single-reed instruments (422.2), the free reeds (412.13) with the free-reed instruments (422.3), and placing the ribbon reeds (412.14) at the end, followed by the category, unrecognised by Hornbostel & Sachs but established by Henry Balfour, of retreating reeds, giving these the new number of 412.15.

FREE AEROPHONES—REEDS—412.1

This section of 412.1, *Idiophonic interruptive aerophones or reeds*, and indeed the whole of 41 *Free Aerophones*, raises very considerable problems. 412.11 *Concussion reeds; two lamellae make a gap which closes periodically during their vibration* and 412.12 *Percussion reeds; a single lamella strikes against a frame* describe the double and single reeds respectively of all our reed instruments as well as those instruments which Hornbostel & Sachs cite in this section.

A further problem arises with just what is a *free aerophone; The vibrating air is not confined by the instrument*. For example, *organ reed stops* are included here, both the ordinary reeds with their pipes (412.1) and the renaissance and early-baroque regals (412.122) with their resonators. With both, the pitch is determined by the vibrating length of the reed, which is fixed by the bridle on the reed, which is presumably why they are classed in this way, but with both, also, the length or the volume of the pipe or resonator must match the pitch of the reed or the coupled system will not function. In addition, it is the shape of the pipe that is the determinant of its tone quality, and thus of the name of that particular rank of reeds or stop. Equally, all the free reed instruments are included here (412.13) even though, with the developed mouthorgans of South-East Asia, the reed will only sound when an air column is coupled to it (hence the fingerhole on these Asian mouthorgans), and in that area the free reed is used, like any other reed, on tubes with fingerholes, which then come under 422.3, among the wind instruments proper.

The logical procedure would be to place each reed type under the appropriate section of 42 (e.g., the concussive [double] reeds under 422.1, the percussive [single] under 422.2, and the free under 422.3, with 422.4 for the ribbon reeds. There could then be separate sections (e.g., 41 and 43 respectively) for the flutes and the trumpets.

CONCUSSION REEDS—412.11

The coiled bark or leaf instrument which, when it is played with a double reed, usually also of bark or leaf, is called a whithorn in English, is known from many other areas. The English name derives from the custom of playing such instruments around the Whitsun (Pentecost) season in spring when the bark is easily detached as the sap rises. Most such instruments, as those below, are also played with a double reed, but coiled bark flutes are known from Norway (IX 4, the *selje fløyte*, a transverse duct harmonic flute), and coiled bark trumpets both from Scandinavia (IX 180, small simple instruments produced in Finland as children's toys) and Brazil. The wide-bore Brazilian instruments cited by Izikowitz (p. 222 ff) are supported with struts of cane or wood tied on externally; the narrow-bored pan-trumpets (ibid.) are to some extent lashed together and thus receive mutual support; what prevents the Scandinavian instruments from collapsing under the necessary pressure of trumpeting is not known. Possibly there should be a wooden mouthpiece. All these instruments are, due to their nature, ephemeral; they are made, used, and then discarded (with the possible exception of the Brazilian pan-trumpets, the examples of which in the Etnografiska Museum in Göteborg have survived for a considerable time without excessive deterioration).

It is probable that the traditional European whithorn, with its long resonator of coiled bark, may belong with the other shawms and oboes (422.1), since the tube may well establish the pitch (only experiment can determine this). The following instruments, however, are all too short to do so, and thus they presumably belong here, although Dr. Picken places his in 422.111.

VI   80   Whithorn, *pībai-maphrāo*, huadong ban village, 25 km from Khon kaen, Central Thailand. Helically coiled coconut leaf "whistle," pinned at the distal end with a sliver of wood; reed missing. No fingerholes. Made by a woman named Mea-khong-mee. Now all-but flattened. L 27.3, W 15.5 × 20, Th 8. Given by Laurence Picken who, in his *Musica Asiatica* article, refers to these as shawms; his is CUMAE 77.415. [φ 14/7/].

A spiral retains the same diameter (e.g., a corkscrew), whereas a helix expands conically (e.g., a gastropod shell). Laurence Picken and I have, for a number of years, made a practice of trying to acquire pairs (or more) of the smaller and less expensive instruments so that we have one for each of us. This is especially our practise with children's toys and similar instruments, in which we are both interested. I benefited greatly from Dr. Picken's world tour, whence came the above and the following instrument as well as many others in my collection. His collection is now in the Cambridge University Museum of Archæology and Ethnography, and their catalogue numbers are cited here for ease of comparison. I was honoured by Dr. Picken with the gift of a Xerox copy of the complete catalogue of that accession.

VI   88   Whithorn, Mohammed Yusof bin Mamai, Tumpai Kelantan Village, Kuala Lumpur, Malaya. Helically coiled leaf "whistle," larger than VI 80, pinned at the distal end with a sliver of wood. No fingerholes. Reed of folded leaf missing. L 93 when measured; with all such instruments, the length depends on the compression of the coils and varies as the instrument is picked up and put down. W 7 × 30, Th 3.5 × 24. Given by Laurence Picken; his CUMAE 77.424. [φ 14/2/41-42].

VIII   134   Whithorn, *mbauli*, Puku People, Coastal region, Cameroons. Helically coiled leaf "whistle," pinned at the distal end with a sliver of wood. No fingerholes. Double reed of folded leaf. Played by children. L 60 + reed (which slides in and out), W 13.5 × 34, Th 5 × 26. Given by Roger Blench, who was one of Dr. Picken's Cambridge students.

REEDPIPES—422

The Hornbostel & Sachs *Systematik* cumulates the reed-blown woodwind, or reedpipes, according to the type of reed, into "422.1 Oboes" with a double (concussion) reed, and "422.2 Clarinets" with a single (percussion) reed. Lower criteria (e.g., 422.111 and 422.112) indicate respectively whether the bore is cylindrical or conical. For three reasons, it would have been more sensible to make the primary criterion that of bore-shape:

1. This has a fundamental acoustical effect on the performance of the instrument.
2. This difference is immediately apparent to the non-expert eye (e.g., to general museum curators), whereas if the reed is missing, it can (e.g., with X 280 and 282 and XI 32 and 34 below) lead to incorrect classification by those who are unfamiliar with the instrument.
3. Certainly since the early-nineteenth century (there is an example of that date by Key of London in the Museum of Welsh Life, St. Fagan's), and possibly earlier, some bassoonists have used a single-reed mouthpiece, such as a miniature clarinet mouthpiece, instead of the more usual double reed, with little or no difference in sound and none in acoustical behaviour. Such mouthpieces are also available today for oboe and cor anglais, though their use on these instruments is rarer than on the bassoon.

The acoustical effect of bore shape is that a cylindrical reed-driven bore behaves as a *stopped pipe*. The pitch is an octave lower than that of a flute of the same length and the instrument will only overblow the odd-numbered harmonics, so that the first overblown note is a twelfth above the fundamental, rather than an octave. Hence, a clarinet, much the same length as a flute, sounds almost an octave lower. A conical reed-driven bore, on the other hand, overblows all the harmonics, so that the first overblown note is an octave above the fundamental. The reason that the oboe does not equate with the flute for pitch and length is that the bore of the oboe, like that of all "conical" reed instruments, is conoidal, rather than truly conical; if the bore were extended to form a true cone (as it is in performance, part way down the player's throat), then an oboe and clarinet of the same true bore length would have lowest notes an octave apart, whereas oboe and flute would sound in unison for the same true bore length.

One reason for the clarinet's slow adoption into music (it was invented around 1700 but it was nearly a century before it was present in every orchestra—Haydn did not score it before his London Symphonies, and Mozart used it in only three symphonies) is because it overblows a twelfth, an arrangement upsetting to players who happily doubled on oboe and transverse flute, whose fingerings were similar enough in the eighteenth century to raise no problems. Not only would players have had to cope with quite different fingerings as soon as the range goes beyond a seventh above the lowest note, but the clarinet required extra keys simply because the human hand does not have enough fingers both to support the instrument and to cover the necessary number of holes to fill the gap of a twelfth nor, save with the smallest instruments, do the hands have a wide enough span.

It cannot be emphasised too strongly that the type of reed is irrelevant to the acoustical behaviour. A cylindrical bore will behave as just described whether the reed is single or double (or free—see the following paragraph), as XI 238a will demonstrate, and as is well-known with the crumhorn, which combines a double reed similar to that of the shawm with a cylindrical bore. A conical bore will also behave as described whether the reed is single or double (or free), as XI 238b will demonstrate, and as is well-known with the conical-bore saxophone with its single reed identical to that of the clarinet, and with the small single-reed mouthpieces available for bassoon, cor anglais, and oboe. Despite these examples, many people are still confused on this issue, which makes it all the more unfortunate that the *Systematik* is arranged as it is.

The third group of reedpipes (422.3), those sounded with a free reed similar to that of the mouth organ and with fingerholes like other reedpipes, is confined to South-East Asia, and experiment has shown that these behave exactly like any other reedpipe, overblowing octaves on conical bores, and twelfths (if at all; few cylindrical-bore reed instruments without a correctly placed speaker-key will overblow at all) on cylindrical bores. It may need emphasis that a free reed will drive a pipe with fingerholes just as well as does a single or double reed. It is "axiomatic" in the mental equipment of the conventionally trained acoustician that a free reed will produce only a single pitch, but such "axioms" are the result of ignorance. The conventionally trained acoustician has no experience of "non-Western" (if one may use this directionally meaningless adjective) music or instruments and thus knows only a very small proportion of the world's instrumentarium. Experiment will show that very few of these "axioms" have any validity outside the normal "Western" orchestras and bands. Even the effects of cylindrical bore on a reed-driven pipe are only valid within quite narrow limits, and experiment shows that a cylindrical pipe that is long enough and narrow enough will behave as though it were conical.

CYLINDRICAL BORE SHAWMS—422.111

III   132k   Paper drinking straws, used to demonstrate double reeds and, with a pair of scissors, that the pitch of a wind instrument depends on the length of its tube. Paper straws blow more easily than plastic (which prefer a very long blade) and, best of all, extra wide bore paper, such as were very kindly sent to me by a lady from America after a demonstration at which I remarked on the increasing difficulty of obtaining paper straws in Britain. A quantity of two different makes, unnumbered because at least one straw is used up at each lecture or other demonstration. Deeko Bendy-Straws (England) L 200, ø 5.5 and Sweetheart Giant Straws (Maryland Paper Products Inc., Baltimore, Md.) L 215, ø 7.4.

XI   258a   Cylindrical piece of aluminium tubing, made by JM for demonstration. Accepts an oboe reed staple (for convenience in demonstrations it is played with a plastic oboe reed) and a single reed made from a goose quill. It is similar in length to a stepped shawm made of three segments of aluminium tubing inserted into each other (XI 258b in 422.112 below), and the pair was constructed to show the different effects of cylindrical and conical reed-driven bores, described above, regardless of the type of reed. The cylindrical example overblows to the twelfth with either reed, and the conical to the octave. I have not yet succeeded in making a free reed of the correct size to drive these air columns. OL 288, bore ø 7.1.

VIII 40 Cylindrical shawm, *balaban*, Iran. Turned boxwood. The bulb at the top is reminiscent of the *holmos* of the Greek *aulos*. Thumb + 7 knife-cut fingerholes, all ø c. 7. With a very large double reed (and a spare) made of a flattened and scraped plant stem. Both reeds have a folded cane bridle and a second bridle to keep the reed closed when not in use. Both reeds seem to have been well used. OL (−22) 327 + reed, (total reed L 119.5), reed socket ø 20.8 × 21, top of bore ø c.12.1, bottom ø 12.2. Bought at Sotheby's, from the World of Islam Exibition, 20/11/1980, lot 193. [φ 1251/32-33, col sl].

The connexion between the *aulos* and the Central Asian shawms such as *balaban* and *mey*, and the Far Eastern such as *guanzi*, *p'iri*, and *hichiriki* is easily demonstrated. Anthony Baines (*Woodwind Instruments*, 202) pointed out that the *hichiriki*, with its seven fingerholes and two thumbholes, was clearly a fusion of two pipes on one, the one with thumb + 3 fingerholes, and the other with thumb + 4. It is generally accepted that the instrument travelled down the Silk Route (see also *LERP*, 585 ff); the question is in which direction? Did it start in Greece, or did it start wherever in Central Asia the Greeks came from? It seems a valid hypothesis that this is yet another of the instruments that can be shown to have started in Central Asia, joining the fiddle bow, the gong, the long trumpet, the *'ud-pipa* style lute and probably others. Why did so many instruments start in this area?

As well as their general shape, these instruments have in common the use of a very large double reed consisting of a wide-bore, cylindrical plant stem flattened at the tip and normally shaved down so that the proximal end has had its cortex removed and is much thinner than the distal end, but with no separation into two distinct blades. The use of a bridle, similar in function to a bassoon reed's wire but made of bamboo, keeps the reed in its proper shape. Greek iconography makes it clear that while some *auloi* used single reeds (as Kathleen Schlesinger established), most used a large double reed which may have been similar to those used on these instruments.

The World of Islam Festival took place in London in 1976 with an exhibition of instruments at the Horniman Museum (see Jean Jenkins & Poul Rovsing Olsen). Instruments had been gathered from all over the Islamic world and those which were surplus to requirement later appeared in a series of sales at Sotheby's where, to my benefit, they attracted little interest.

VI   118   Cylindrical shawm, *mey*, Turkey. White wood, black painted. Thumb + 7 drilled fingerholes, all ø c. 5.5. The bulb at the top is reminiscent of the *holmos* of the Greek *aulos*. OL (−c. 40) 345 + reed (total reed L 109), reed socket ø15.7, conical to the top of the bore, ø c. 11.1, bottom ø 11. Kindly brought back from Turkey for me by David Kilpatrick who bought it from a player. The large double reed, similar to that of the *balaban*, began to disintegrate and I was brought another one, apparently from a different plant, L 116.2, which is now disintegrating in its turn. For full information on the *mey*, its reed, and its playing technique, see *LERP*, 475 ff. [φ 14/5/32-33, col sl; reed 14/3].

I   196   Cylindrical shawm, *guanzi*, China, wood with low-melting-point metal resembling pewter or lead run into the wood as decoration. Thumb + 7 fingerholes, 10.8 × 8.6, th 10.2 × 8.6, 10.8 × 8.2, 10.4 × 8.5, 10.2 × 8.4, 10 × 8.1, 10.1 × 8.1, 9.8 × 7.5. The three lower fingerholes are closer together than the four upper. Only the thumbhole, and the slight evasion of the bore to form a reed socket, indicate which end is the top. The reed, while large, is clearly a different plant from those of the *mey* and *balaban* and has a wire binding towards the distal end; it has not been scraped. OL (−7.3) 251 + reed (total reed L 55.9), reed socket ø 15.7, the metal slightly scraped to form a cone 7.3 deep (the depth of the metal), then bore ø c. 14, bottom 14.9. Bought from Collet's Chinese Bookshop. One of a batch of Chinese instruments that had been ordered by Peter Crossley-Holland but arrived (I think by some years) too late to be of use to him—in those days, the early 1960s, such things were not easily obtainable in England. [φ 1284/2/5-6 and b/w slide].

VII 166   Two cylindrical shawms, *guanzi*, China. Bamboo. Thumb + 7 fingerholes, all ø 9 × 8.5. One short (a), OL 194 + reed, bore ø top 11.3, bottom 12.5. This wider end would clearly be the top, slightly evased as a reed well, if the instrument were inverted, with the thumbhole below the fingerholes instead of above them. The other long (b), OL 346 + reed, bore ø top 9.9 × 10.5, bottom 10.9 × 11.5, which might also be a reed well. They could be played that way up: the lower thumb can then reach the dorsal hole. Bought from Raymond Man, Covent Garden with 2 spare reeds. [φ 1249].

Raymond Man has a shop for Chinese musical instruments in Covent Garden, London; he also stocks some Indian and other instruments. He always stocks suitable reeds, strings, and other accessories, and reeds for many of the instruments in this catalogue were bought from him.

VIII 176 Cylindrical shawm, *guanzi*, China, made of pale green jade. Eight fingerholes, all ø c. 6.1. No thumbhole. It is probably a votive instrument or for deposit in a grave rather than intended as a practicable instrument. OL 365 + reed, bore ø top 14.2 tapering for 17 mm to ø 12, and then more gradually for 65 to ø 11.4, bottom 11.3. Bought at Sotheby's 5/11/1981, lot 45, where it was catalogued as "Ti tzu . . . membrane hole and embouchure absent," i.e., a flute (*di*) which was broken so that part of its length was missing. A glance showed that it was unbroken and its true identity was obvious, but fortunately not to anyone else, so that it cost very little.

X 226 Cylindrical shawm, *guan*, China, small bamboo, square section externally, with a small black double-reed cut to a point and without a ligature. Five burned fingerholes, all ø c. 4.2, no thumbhole. OL 110 + reed (total reed L 5.7), bore ø 5.5, ext 7.4. Brought back and given by Helen Rees.

I 194 Cylindrical shawm, *hichiriki*, Japan, the instrument of the *gagaku* orchestra. Bamboo, bound with willow bark in traditional patterns. Two thumb + 7 fingerholes, 9 × 5.1, th 8 × 5, 8.9 × 5, 8.1 × 4.7, 8.3 × 4.5, th 8.2 × 4.5, 8.2 × 4.5, 7.9 × 4.3, 7.7 × 4.3, all a narrow, sharply pointed oval. With a spare reed and silk bag. OL 186 + reed (total reed L 57), reed socket ø c. 16, contracts conically to bore ø 11.9 at top fingerhole, 10.7 at foot. Reed lapped with paper to fit socket, with bamboo ligature and cap to hold it closed. Kindly brought back by Professor Ronald Dore who bought it for me in Tokyo. [φ 1284/2/2-4 and b/w slide].

X   60   Cylindrical shawm, *hichiriki*, Japan. A modern instrument
                made in plastic but exactly simulating the original, includ-
                ing the appearance of the binding, in a plastic case. The
                reed is natural reed, not plastic. Two thumb + 7 finger-
                holes, 8.5 × 4.5, th 9.2 × 4.6, 8.5 × 4.9, 8.8 × 4.5, 7.7 ×
                5, th 7.9 × 4, 8 × 4.8, 8 × 5.1, 8 × 4.6, all more smoothly
                oval. OL 183, reed socket ø 14.2 × 15, contracts conically
                to bore ø 11.2 at top fingerhole, 10.2 at foot. Kindly
                brought back for me and given by Tony Bingham.

    Tony Bingham is London's most important dealer in antique and ex-
otic instruments, now in Pond Street, Hampstead, though in Poland Street
in the West End when I first started buying from him. Much of my collection has been bought from him over the years.

I   64   Approximations to ancient Egyptian *māt*, made JM. Two
                brass tubes of differing length, of diameter that will accept
                an oboe staple. The longer with thumb + 3 fingerholes, the
                shorter with thumb + 2, all ø 4.6, drilled with a 3/16" bit
                and lightly countersunk. The longer OL 550, the shorter
                OL 350, bore of each ø 7.0. These were made simply to
                demonstrate the type; they are not intended to be true re-
                productions and there has been no attempt to approximate
                the bores or other aspects of surviving pipes either in di-
                ameter or length. [φ 1234/B/21-22].

VI   248   Tenor crumhorn, Germany, marked: GÜNTER / KORBER.
                Very approximate reconstruction of a renaissance instru-
                ment. The plastic reed, screw-controlled by a pressure pad
                on each side, is in a windcap. Thumb + 7 fingerholes +
                non-authentic key for upper forefinger + 2 vents, ø key 2.3,
                th 2.9, 3, 3, 3.3, wide gap, 3, 3.6, 3.3, offset for R little fin-
                ger 3.5, vents 4, 3.8. OL 645, total L 860, reed socket ø 9.3,
                bore L (−32.5 ø 6.5) 750; bell 22 × 23, contracting to the
                bore diameter 7 over c. 28 mm. Bought from James Tyler.
                [φ 1236/2-3].

    Korber's crumhorns are based on those designed by Otto Steinkopf
which, even though he was chief conservator at the Berlin Hochschule
Musikinstrumenten Museum, bear little resemblance in bore diameter, fingerhole diameter, sound volume, or tone quality to any original instru-

ments; this is one of Korber's later models and considerably better than the earlier, but still without any great resemblance to originals. They are still designed to work with a plastic reed. Anthony Moonen's article in *GSJ* demonstrates the morphological differences; iconographic evidence from the period (e.g., *The Triumph of Maximilian*, pl. 20 in the Dover edition) shows that crumhorns could be used with loud instruments such as shawms, and that therefore they cannot have been the feeble, buzzing instruments we mostly know today. See also Barra Boydell.

CONICAL BORE SHAWMS—422.112

This, of course, is the classic shawm; the cylindrical-bore shawms are limited in range, both in the musical and the geographical senses. The question is when did the conical shawm first appear? The first evidence for it so far discovered, leaving aside the mysterious double pipes of the Neolithic marble figures from the Cycladic Isles, some of which appear to be conical, is a Faliscan bowl, dating from around 480 B.C., with a scene portraying the contest of Apollo and Marsyas; the Faliscans were a sub-tribe of the Etruscans. The bowl is now in the collections of Stanford University and is illustrated by Heinz Becker, Abb. 3. Marsyas is holding a pair of instruments, one in each hand, with large reeds with bridles like those of the *mey*, *balaban*, and *hichiriki*. The exterior of each instrument is clearly conical, but there is no way of telling whether the interior is also. There seems little point, however, in taking the trouble to carve or turn a conical exterior unless the bore is to be conical also. The same applies to a number of later Etruscan and Roman illustrations such as those published by Fleischhauer (e.g., Abb. 4, 11, 37). Then comes something of a gap in the evidence, the next illustration being on a well-known eighth- to ninth-century A.D. Sassanid silver vessel in the Musée des Beaux Arts in Lyons, illustrated by Farmer in the same series (Abb. 7–9), which shows a clearly conical shawm, an harp, a Chinese mouth organ, a form of *'ud* strongly resembling a Chinese *pipa*, and an hourglass drum.

Presumably due to the antipathy to illustration in the Islamic world, there is then a further gap until the thirteenth century, whereafter there is a plethora of illustration in European mediæval manuscripts, from the *Cántigas de Santa Maria* onward and, in England, the *Luttrell* and *Gorleston Psalters*. Therefore the shawm can be taken as an indication of contact with the Islamic world wherever it appears. The assumption is that the instrument persisted in the Persian and Arab world from the classical period and was encountered and brought back to Europe by the invading Crusaders. An illustration in *The Luttrell Psalter* (BL Add Ms 42130, f. 164v, illustrated in my *Medieval & Renaissance*, pl. 38) specifically associates the shawm with Constantinople and shows it being played there. It also travelled from the Maghrib through Iberia across the Pyrenees. It became the leading melodic instrument for loud music throughout mediæval Europe from the fourteenth to the mid-seventeenth century, when it vanished from the mainstream of European art music with the need for a quieter indoor double-reed instrument and resulting in invention of the oboe in France or Holland. It survives worldwide in all Islamic areas, and in many areas which have been in contact with Islam, even indirectly as in México, whither it was taken by the Conquistadors, and sometimes only in its bag-blown form, as today in the Scottish Highlands.

The route, or source, of transmission can, to some extent, be traced by the instrument's name, for there are two groups of names, one the eastern Arabic *zūrnā* group and the other the western Arabic or Maghribi *ghaita* group. *Zūrnā* led to *śahnāī, suona, sarune, bnè,* perhaps also to *shawm,* and *ghaita* led to *algaita, gaida, wait,* and so forth. Alastair Dick has shown that some Indian shawms derived from classical and Middle Eastern originals, such as those noted here, in pre-Islamic times, before the Moghul invasions.

The shawm's characteristic playing technique is with the reed pouched wholly in the mouth, leading to a loud and penetrating sound, rich in overtones, which in some places is ameliorated by drilling a set of vents in the bell, known in some areas as devil-holes because they let the devil out. In a few areas the reed is lipped, especially, for example, in North-Indian art music today with the *śahnāī,* which seems to be the first stage toward the re-invention of the oboe, for inhibiting the freedom of vibration of the reed with the lips reduces the loudness and the upper overtones very considerably. This technique can also be heard on recordings by mediæval and other early-music ensembles where, to avoid overloading the microphone, players made the shawm sound like a coarse cor anglais by lipping the reed. The use of circular breathing is normal in almost all areas, as it is with single-reed pipes and other wind instruments; the player alternates blowing from the diaphragm with blowing out from the cheeks while breathing in through the nose; hence the occasional use of the term cheek-pumping for this technique. See 422.112.21 (bagpipes) below for further detail on this.

Reeds vary in type. The Turkish reed is a flattened aquatic plant stem, and it and its manufacture have been described in great detail by Laurence Picken (*LERP*, 356 ff). The reed in the Maghrib and in China, as well as in parts of India and Tibet (where the term "mud-grass" was recorded by Colonel Montagu Cleeve, whose Tibetan shawms are in the Bate Collection), is also a flattened plant stem. All are a flattened stem without any division into separate blades, and thus are quite different from the normal European shawm reed, which is a scraped length of *arundo donax*, or a similar hard cane, made into two blades, usually on much the same principle as the oboe or bassoon reed. A few shawms, for example the smaller Batak type, X 282 and XI 34 in 422.212 below, and the Hungarian shawms made of gourd noted by Bálint Sárosi (p. 85), have a single reed, in the Hungarian case of goose quill. A group of South-East Asian shawms, such as the Thai *pī*, the Burmese *hnè*, and some others, have multiplex reeds, usually said to be of palm leaf, with two, three, or even four layers of leaf on either side of the wind channel.

The simplest conical shawm is a stepped cone such as Nazir Jairazbhoy found and recorded in Andhra Pradesh (*A Musical Journey*, ex. 7:2), a series of bamboo segments of different diameters, each stepped into the next. This is just as effectively conical, so far as its acoustical behaviour is concerned, as a true cone and is, of course, much simpler to produce.

XI   258b   Stepped shawm, made JM of three segments of aluminium tubing for demonstration. The narrowest segment accepts an oboe reed staple (for convenience in demonstrations it is played with a plastic oboe reed) and a single reed made of a goose quill. The segments, each of a different bore diameter, are stepped into each other and are held together with adhesive gaffer tape. It is similar in length to a single length of aluminium tubing which is the same bore as the narrowest of the segments (XI 258a in 422.111), and the pair was constructed to show the different effects of cylindrical and conical reed-driven bores regardless of the type of reed. The conical example overblows to the octave with either reed, whereas the cylindrical overblows to a twelfth. OL 282, narrow bore L 88, ø 7.1; medium bore L 133, ø 11; wide bore L 61, ø 13.

Forked Shawms

The stepped fork, which is known only from the area of the extended Ottoman Empire, from Macedonia to Armenia, to the Caucasus, to Persia, to Morocco, is clearly a fairly recent invention, within perhaps the last two centuries, and represents a considerable ergological improvement in manufacture over the conventional conical bore because it avoids the necessity for conical reamers and other more elaborate tools. It allows the main bore to be cylindrical, so that it can be bored by a normal drill or even by a hot iron, save for the bell-flare, which is easily shaped with a knife. The conical metal staple, on which the reed is placed, is followed by the three "cylindrical" diameters of the fork. The first is the initial tube through the head of the fork; the second is the wider tube formed by the first opening opposite the uppermost fingerhole; the third is the wider bore still formed by the second opening opposite the thumbhole. This third "cylinder" between the tines of the fork leads into the body of the instrument, sometimes with a short conical step since the points of the tines of the fork are often cut conically, either or both from side to side and from interior to exterior. This is normally the narrowest point of the body bore, for the top of the body is evased slightly to admit the fork. These four steps, the staple and the three stages of the fork, form a stepped cone which suffices to make the bore effectively conical. Cylindrical and cylinder are in quotes above because, while each step of the bore is usually much the same diameter at top and bottom, the shape is not really that of a cylinder, being considerably wider from front to back, from thumbhole to fingerholes, than it is from side to side. I am not sure what term should be used for a parallelogram with rounded ends—jujube-shape? See fig. 1a for a sketch of the fork in section, and fig. 1b for the same fork inserted into the head of a shawm.

It is clear from Carpaccio's paintings of *The Turkish Ambassadors in Venice* and one of his St. George paintings, and from a very old instrument in the Picken Collection (*LERP*, plate 41*n*) now CUMAE 77/55, that the Turkish shawm was originally conical throughout, even if not lathe-turned (see, for example V 186 below, which also is conical though not lathe-turned); the fork must have been devised at a later date than that of Picken's instrument. See a brief paper of mine in *FoMRHIQ* 21. Longer and more detailed conference papers were given at SEEM a València 2 in 1992, and, in 1996, in Oxford at the Maison Française ICTM conference on Arabic and Beduin music; an expanded version of the latter is published in the ICTM's *Yearbook for Traditional Music* for 1997.

While the forked shawm is found today over the whole area of what was the Ottoman Empire, no evidence has as yet been found of its origin at any point in that area. Dr. Eckhard Neubauer made the cogent point at the Maison Française conference that so important a technological development was much more likely to have been made at the centre than at the periphery and that the fact that the shawm was the most important melodic instrument of the Janissary Band would tend to emphasise this. However, no evidence has as yet been discovered.

NB: Some nonsense has been written about the fork being a transposing device because rotating it closes the uppermost fingerhole. A moment's thought shows that closing the *uppermost* fingerhole cannot affect the basic pitch nor the key in which it plays.

VIII   44   Shawm, *ghaita*, Morocco. With a stepped fork in the head. Thumb + 7 fingerholes, all ø c. 6.5, + 7 vents (devil holes), all ø c. 4, which are bored horizontally and then cut downwards. The vents on all these forked shawms, except for XI 36 a and b and VIII 36, are arranged in an I pattern, an horizontal row of 3, then a single hole below the central one of those, and then another row of 3. The top right vent is stopped with a plug which projects into the bore. The bell is covered with a tin-plate (ferrous) garland to repair a crack which is covered with wax internally. The head of the fork is chipped and the wood of the fork is thin and broken at one point; it was lapped by a piece of thin red cotton which has been removed because it was too tight. An old instrument. OL 404 + staple (all overall lengths here ignore the staple because there is no way to be certain how far it should go into the socket), fork internal length (−42) 129; socket ø 11.1 cylindrical with a pronounced step to top of bore ø 6.8 for 16.4 long; first opening ø 6.5 × 9.8, 14.2 long; second opening ø 6.00 × bore ø, 64 long; body bore tapers from top ø 17.5 to 15.4 level with the thumbhole. The interior of the bell is clearly knife cut, ø 83.3, 89 ext. From the World of Islam Exhibition, marked Morocco 33. Bought at Sotheby's (who lost the staple and reed during the sale; it was there when viewed and has now been re-placed), 20/11/1980, lot 198. [φ 1251/28-29].

IX   188   Shawm, *ghaita*, Morocco. Stepped fork in the head. Thumb + 7 fingerholes, all ø 8, + 7 vents, all ø c. 5, all slop-ing sharply downwards. The staple has a support for a pirou-ette but pirouettes were said by the vendor to be only neces-sary for those without teeth; one of Picken's informants amplified this by saying (*LERP*, 507) that the pirouette's function was not to support the lips but to prevent the in-strument being pushed down the player's throat by collision with a dancer or bystander. With original carrying bag. Bell decorated with incised rings. Fork was lapped with a small piece of paper, removed for safety. OL 393, fork internal L (−45.6) 130, socket ø 11.1, top of bore ø 6.2 for 8.7 long; first opening (square cut) ø 7.4 × 11, 14.3 long; second open-ing (round cut) ø 7.7 × bore ø for 62; body bore tapers from top ø16.5 to 15.8; bell lathe turned, ø 70.4, 74 ext. Bought in the *shuk* in Agadir from an instrument maker. [φ col sl].

III   188   Shawm, *ghaita*, Morocco. Stepped fork in the head. Box-wood. Thumb + 7 fingerholes all 7.5 + 7 vents all c. 5.5 sloping downwards. Brass dentated bell garland as on the European shawm. Large bone pirouette; the hole in the cen-tre has lateral slots to pass over the reed, but the staple does not have a pirouette rest. OL 395, staple is now fixed (L incl staple 431) but whether it is glued or only jammed is not vis-ible; it seems not to be thread-lapped but to be directly metal to wood. Fork internal L (−57.6) 129, bore through fork apparently conical, ø at distal end 6.5; first opening ø 7.5 × 8.9 for 13 long; second opening ø 8.1 × bore ø for 64.5; body bore tapers from top ø 17.5 to 16.4; bell 63.2, ext 73.6. Pirouette ø 60 × 56.5. Bought from an antique shop in Ostend during the IFMC Conference there in 1967. On loan to the Bate Collection (*x 2024*), where it is shown "ex-ploded" so that the fork may be seen. [φ 1234/C/34-36; 1284/2/9-10; b/w slide, col sl incl detail of fork].

The Bate Collection, of which I was curator from 1981 until I re-tired in 1995, is in the Faculty of Music of the University of Oxford; a hundred or two of my instruments are still there on loan, and those relevant are noted here.

VII 22 Shawm, *zurna*, Turkey. Stepped fork in the head. Thumb + 7 fingerholes, all ø 5.3, + 7 vents, all ø 4.5. Black painted apricot wood. Pirouette of yellow plastic marked A. FIRDAN, with a slot for the reed to pass through. Smooth curve to bell flare, slight flare to head. The Turkish shawms have a much sharper bell flare than the Moroccan. OL 337, fork internal L (−41) 86, socket ø 9.2, tapering, then ø 5.7 for 5 long; first opening ø 4.8 × 7.2 for 14; second opening 5.2 × bore ø for 36 to 43 (the tines have pointed ends); body bore tapers from top ø 13.2 to 11.5, bell lathe turned, ø 90.7, 98.5 ext. Bought new in a street market in Istanbul by Tony Bingham; Hamdi Ataoglu bought a staple, pirouette, and reeds on my behalf when he was in London working with Lucille Armstrong. [φ 1238; col sl].

XI 36a/b Two shawms, *zurna*, Turkey. (a) is larger and paler wood than (b). Stepped fork in the heads. Both with thumb + 7 fingerholes, (a) all ø 6.2; (b) all ø 6, + only 3 very small vents, (a) ø 2.8, (b) ø 3, in a straight horizontal line. Both with 3 incised and stained rings round the head of the fork. Both with staple and reed but not pirouette, which was said to be made by the player, often from a coin. Both with a smooth curve to the bell flare and a slight flare to the head.

a) OL 315, fork internal L (−27) 77; socket ø 9.6, conical to ø 5.8 for 8 long; first opening ø 7.9 × 7.2 for 12 long; second opening ø 6.7 × bore ø for 31 long, but the points of the tines bend inwards and are only 4 mm apart at their ends; body bore tapers from top ø 11.8 to 11.3, bell ø 74.6, 84.6 ext. [φ col sl].

b) The smaller of the two, made of darker wood. OL 272, fork internal L 60; socket ø 8.5, tapering over 8.1 to slight step and contracting further over 21 to ø 5.7 for 14 long; first opening ø 5.5 × 7.5 for 13.4 long; second opening ø 6.5 × bore ø for 26 long; body bore tapers from topø 12 to 11.4, bell ø 63.2, 72.7 ext. Both were kindly brought back by and bought from Captain Steve

Gaherty of the USAF while he was supervising arrangements for feeding Kurds in Northern Iraq after the Gulf War.

IV   162   Treble Shawm, *zurla*, Macedonia. Pair of shawms, treble and tenor (IV 160), which are used together. Whitish unstained wood. Stepped fork in the heads. Thumb + 7 fingerholes, ø 6.5 × 5.7, th 6 × 5.7, 6 × 5.8, 6.2 × 6, 6.5, 6.8 × 6.5, 7 × 6.4, 6.5 × 6.2, + 7 vents, ø varying from 5.5 to 6.5. Each with a sheet-metal pirouette soldered to the staple. Fragments of broken reed on each. Old well-used instruments. OL 278, fork internal L (−37) 60; socket ø 9, tapering to 5.5 for 8 long; first opening ø 5.1 × 7.7 for 9.8 long, second opening ø 5.7 × bore ø for 21, body bore tapers from top ø 14.9 to 9.9 below third fingerhole, bell ø 68.9, 76 ext. Bought from Vasily Hadjimanov, Skopje, after he visited us in 1967 after the Ostend IFMC Conference.[φ 1234/I/3-5; b/w sl].

IV   160   Tenor shawm, *zurla*, Macedonia. See description of IV 162. Interior of the bell painted black. Fingerholes clearly burned, all ø 8; vents vary from 7 to 8, depending on the thickness of the wood, which is greater (and the holes therefore narrower) towards the bell. OL 545, fork internal L (−58.5) 118, socket ø 14.5 tapering to ø 8 for 22.5 long; first opening ø 6.5 × 11.3 for 18.5; second opening ø 6 × bore ø for 43 long; body bore tapers from top ø 20.2 to 16.2 level with third fingerhole, bell ø 83.7, 98.8 ext. [φ 1234/B/25-26; 1234/Z/23, col sl].

VIII   36   Shawm, *mizmar*, Assiut, Egypt. Stepped fork in the head. Thumb + 7 fingerholes all fairly rough, ø mostly about 6.5, but thumb and the two lowest only 5.5, + 9 vents in 3 rows of 3, even rougher but all around 4 ø. The body is covered with a leather sleeve, an animal tail or leg for there is no seam, a brass collar, crudely soldered at the back, covering its top. Below the sleeve there is a plated metal ring and then a narrow rubber ring. A blank plated metal plaque is nailed to the bell. A metal (perhaps zinc but more probably aluminium) garland over the end of the bell covers a crack which has been glued and stapled; it is possible that the leather sleeve does so also. OL 343, fork internal L (−42) 96, socket ø 11.6 tapering to 6.5 for 12 long; first opening ø 6.2 × 10 for 14.5; second opening ø 6.7 × bore ø for 46.7 long; body bore tapers from top ø 16.5 to 13.4; bell ø c. 83, c. 91 ext. Bought from Gwen Plumley who bought it in Assiut for me, with seven spare reeds in a tin which she bought in Cairo "from the players in the folk band at the Meridien Hotel." [φ 1251/30-31; col sl].

XII   118   Shawm, found uncatalogued. Thumb + 7 fingerholes, all ø 5.5, + 7 vents, all ø 5.1. All the holes are neatly drilled, with sharp edges, and show no signs of charring, unlike many of those above. The cylindrical head, which has turned decoration, is not flared like the Turkish shawms above; the devil holes are drilled horizontally, like the Turkish, not sloping downwards like the Moroccan. The bell shape is more like the Moroccan but has a bead above the rim. The wood, of no great quality, is dark-stained. The staple has no pirouette support, unlike most of the other forked shawms here. The fork is quite short. OL 344, fork internal L (−28) 76, socket ø 9 tapering to 6 for 25.5 long; first opening ø 6.5 × 8 for 12 long; second opening ø 6.5 × bore ø; body bore tapers from top ø 13 to 12.1; bell ø 66.3, 52.7 ext. I have a faint memory of buying this in Tangier, but this cannot be confirmed.

Carved Bore Shawms

On these instruments the bore is conical and has been carved by hand, rather than turned on a lathe. Because the Nigerian instruments are covered with a sleeve of leather, details of their construction are difficult to ascertain, but they seem to be made of one piece of wood (plus a long, conical, metal staple), the narrowly conical body integral with the bottle-shape bell. Shawms in West Africa are used mainly by the Hausa and the other Muslim peoples of the neighbouring countries and it is assumed that they were acquired as they passed through the Maghrib on their way from further east to their present locations. The name of the shawm, *algaita*, is one of the indicators of this. Morphologically, the instrument differs considerably from the Maghribi *ghaita* used today, but this is not unexpected, for the stay of the Hausa and Fulani in the Maghrib is much earlier than the invention of the forked shawm. It is possible that this is what the Maghribi shawm was like some centuries ago, though the presence of an amulet beneath the leather of I 192 is likely to be a Nigerian feature.

I   192   Shawm, *algaita*, Hausa Nigeria. Carved conical bore. Red leather covered 'wood' with a long metal staple missing. Thumb + 4 fingerholes cut through the stitched leather cover, the thumb and first fingerhole, opposite each other, well above the others and close to the top, ø th 7.5, 8.1, 11.7 × 9.1, 10.5 × 9.4, 10.1 × 9.1. A small hole, ø 4.5, drilled in the side of the bell. There is an amulet between the leather cover and the wood at the top of the bell, aligned with the fingerholes. The leather is lightly incised with decorative patterns throughout. Body L 337, socket ø 16 tapering to 13.9, bore at top of bell c. 28, bell 61 × 64, 68.8 × 71.6 ext. From the Evan Thomas Collection, no. 759 (according to a paper label inside the bell), bought from Page Phillips, Kensington Church Street. [φ 1284/2, col sl].

V   182   Shawm, *algaita*, Zaria, Nigeria. Carved conical bore. Thumb + 4 fingerholes. The uppermost fingerhole and the thumbhole are again opposite each other and well separated from the other three fingerholes, but are much further from the top of the instrument than with I 192. ø th 7, 9, 9.3, 9.5, 9.5. Only partly leather covered, down to the top of the bell. This example seems to be made of wood, but I 192 and XII 120 (and from memory V 184) appear to be made of palm or some similar more fibrous material. The top 37 mm is a separate piece of wood inserted into the top, stopping level with the upper finger- and thumbholes. Holes are burned through the leather. Recent instrument made for me in Zaria. Body L 378, staple and reed L 139, socket ø c. 12.5 tapering to 8.4 at the base of the insert, bore at top of bell c. 23, bell 52.5 × 54.5, 65.6 × 67.5 ext. Bought through the Gidan Madauchi Zazzau Ibrahim Bagudu of Zaria City. [φ 6260/ 11/2-3].

By an introduction from Professor David Ames, initially to ascertain for him whether the *til'boro*, one of the side-blown single-reed instruments (VI 48 in 422.22), had a beating reed or a free reed (it is beating), I was able to obtain many Hausa instruments through the Madauchi.

V   184   Shawm, *algaita*, Hausa Nigeria. Staple missing. An older leather covered instrument, rougher than I 192. The leather over the body is poor in quality; that over the bell is darker and better. Carved conical bore. Thumb + 4 fingerholes knife cut (or haggled) through the leather and the wood (not measured); the thumbhole is drilled and is smaller in diameter. Body L 312 mm; socket ø 16 × 17; bell internal ø 59, external 67. Bought in an antique shop in Blackheath. Not found when this catalogue was being compiled (October, 1996). Some duplicate instruments have been given to colleagues without this being recorded. [φ 6260/11/6-7].

XII   120   Shawm, *algaita*, Muslim West Africa. Acquired a number of years ago but not then catalogued because it was very badly wormed; it was then sealed into a polythene bag for safety and later frozen to kill any remaining insects. Five fingerholes, ø c. 7.6, 8.2, 7.5, 7.5, 7.5, and no thumbhole, all rough cut through leather and wood. The top 71 mm is a separate piece of wood and includes the uppermost fingerhole, which is, as usual, well separated from the others; the lowest is blocked with a stopper made of a piece of gourd. The body is covered in brown leather, the bell in red. A long metal staple, also leather covered, is attached to the body by a leather ribbon. The greater length and different fingerhole pattern suggests that this is not Nigerian but from a neighbouring country with a similar Muslim culture. Body L 404, staple and reed L 138, bore ø top 15.6, at top of bell c. 19, end of bell 61 × 65, 70 × 74 ext. Perhaps acquired with other material in a lot at a Sotheby "World of Islam" sale.

VII   232   Shawm, perhaps Italy. Carved, not turned, with a brass collar over the proximal end which is sharply shouldered at that point. Roughly made, the plane of the bell end is not at right angles to that of the body length. Black painted white wood. Six fingerholes, ø 5.9 × 6.7, 5.7, 5.3, 6.8, 5.8, 5.8 (no thumbhole) which are not in a straight line. The fingerholes are all quite roughly cut and most are conical through the wood; it is interesting how, nevertheless, they are so uniform in size, save for the uppermost, and shows that the instrument was made with greater care than its general appearance might suggest. Staple missing. A copper wire was twisted round the body in a groove between the third and fourth fingerholes before the instrument was painted. OL (−24) 252, socket ø 15.5, tapering to 12.6. The bell flares over the final 30 mm or so from ø c. 17 to c. 41.5, 52.8 × 54 ext. Bought from Tony Bingham who had bought it with a box of other material, most of which was Italian; hence the attribution. However, VII 234 which was acquired from the same source at the same time, is almost certainly Mexican; the two instruments are quite different in all respects but length and the fact that both are carved, not turned. [φ 1250].

VII   234   Shawm, *chirimía*, Oaxaca, Southern México (see Joan Rimmer, Chirimia, fig. 3c). Carved, not turned. Roughly made of quite rough wood. 7 fingerholes, all ø c. 5.5, + 2 vents ø 3.4, burned in. First fingerhole is very high, which must make it difficult to insert the staple, now missing, which would have been long enough to render the instrument acoustically conical. A narrow raised ring between the lowest fingerhole and the vents marks the beginning of the slight bell flare. OL 258, socket ø 14.5 tapering to 11.5 after c. 170mm, bore above bell 12, flares over final 30 mm or so to bell ø c. 30, 36.5 ext. Given by Tony Bingham. [φ 1251/10-11].

V   186   Shawm, *chirimía*, Isthmus of Tuantepec, México. Carved conical bore with a large separate wooden bell. Made in imitation of a renaissance Spanish instrument. Six fingerholes apparently burned in, ø 6.7, 7, 6, 7, 7.5, 7.5; incised rings between the holes. Long metal staple (c. 150 mm) missing. OL 368, socket ø 16.5 tapering to c. 14, body L 209 (+20 ø c. 24), bell ø 101 × 108, 117 × 120 ext, ht c. 150. Bought from Maurice Byrne who bought it from a stall in the Portobello Road. [φ 6260/11/10-12].

VII   86   Treble shawm, Laurence Wright, Llanfairpwll. Seven fingerholes, ø 4.8, 7.3, 5.8, 6.4, 6.4, 6.7, 6.4, lowest offset for right little finger, high on the instrument (360 from the lowest to the end of the bell), 3 dorsal vents, ø 4.8. With a wooden spool pirouette. Reconstruction of the late mediæval type. It should have a reamed conical bore but it was made by splitting, gouging, and reuniting one piece of wood because Laurence Wright did not have a lathe. Made for me. OL (− 19 ø 4.8) 660, socket for pirouette ø 9.5; bell ø c. 28 before final 70 mm of flare to 112.5 ext. [φ 1247].

Reamed Bore Shawms

These, like most of the forked shawms above and unlike the carved shawms, appear to have been turned on a lathe. They differ from the forked shawms in that the bore is conical and has presumably been formed with one or more reamers, tapering tools which have their cutting edge along the side and which are forged or lathe-turned to a profile which is the shape of the bore or of a part thereof. A cylindrical pilot bore is drilled down the bore first, and one or more reamers then follow this and cut the bore into a cone.

I   174   Shawm, *bombarde*, Rennes, Brittany. Reamed conical bore. Cheap modern instrument designed to be used with the *biniou braz*, the Breton version of the Highland Great Pipes. Wood with plastic ferrules and bell ring. Separate bell. 6 fingerholes + key, ø 4.3, 4.3, 4.3, 4.3, 5.3, 5.3, key 7.9. The reed of *arundo donax* is formed like a small bagpipe-chanter reed with a conical cork ferrule. OL 307, socket ø 7, body L (−16 ø 4.6) 275 (+13 ø 17); bell ø 46.5 int, 73 ext. Bought in a music shop in Quimper with a tutor by Jean L'Helgouach which illustrates this type of bombarde with a key. [φ 1241; b/w slide].

IX   94   Shawm, *bombarde*, Brittany. Blackwood. Seven fingerholes, ø 4.2, 5.4, 5.4, 4.5, 5.7, 5.7, 5.5, the lowest offset for R little finger. Detachable bell of the same wood. Presumably a rather older tradition than I 174, and a much better quality

instrument, but whether this is the older *bombarde*, used
with the *vrai biniou* is doubtful. The reed is the same pattern as that of I 174. OL 277, body L 222 (+18 ø 13.4),
socket ø 8, tapering to top of bore 4.2; bell ø 54.5 int, 63.5
ext. Bought from the Bath Early Music Shop at an Early Instrument Exhibition at the Horticultural Hall. [φ col sl].

I   186   Shawm, *dolçaina*, València. Reamed conical bore of a wide taper with a brass staple which also expands rapidly. Thumb +
7 fingerholes, ø th and 4 highest 7.2, 9.7 × 9, 7.2, 5.9 (lowest offset to right) + 2 lateral vents, ø 10. Uses an unusually
large reed of a softish material which does not look like
arundo donax but which nevertheless is made in two blades.
OL (−17 ø 8.8) 300, socket ø 13.5, bell ø 54, 67 ext. Bought
from Michael Morrow. A second, given by Gordon Harris,
missing its staple and with a cracked and glued bell, was ex-
changed with Herbert Myers for two examples of his proto-
type of the Korber renaissance transverse flute, one of which
is IV 32 in 421.121.120; the other was given to Philip Bate
and is now in the Bate Collection (*x 125)*. [φ1241].

XI   100   Shawm, *dolçaina*, València. Reamed conical bore. Thumb +
7 fingerholes, ø th and 4 highest 8.1, 9.5, 8.1, 5.8, the lowest offset to the right, + 2 lateral vents, ø 9.5. Slightly
larger, and better wood than I 186; a much better quality
instrument but otherwise similar. With four reeds, of
arundo donax formed on metal staples like wide oboe reeds,
in a cigarette box. The staples are brass and quite thick and
solid. OL (−18.5 ø 9.7) 303, socket ø 13; bell ø 55 int, 68
ext. Presented to me by Vicent Torrent during SEEM a
València 2 at Alacant, September 1992. While there, I
bought a tutor by Xavier Ahuir Cardells.

XI   170   Shawm, *gralla sec*, Xavier Auriols, Vilanova, Catalunya.
Marked PALAMERAR / [leaf pattern] / VILANOVA. Thumb +
6 fingerholes in a straight line, ø 6.3, th 6.8, 6.7, 6.7, 6.7,
10.4, 8.7, + 2 lateral vents ø 9.1. Metal mount round the
top and two round the bell where the wood started to crack,
but see the description of the Basque *dultzaina*, XII 146,
which suggests that these mounts may be part of the basic

design. The *gralla* is the characteristic shawm of the north of Catalunya, the *dolçaina* of the Pais València to the south. These are the standard folk instruments, whereas the *tiple* and *tenora* of the *sardana coblas*, which are shawms with oboe-like key work, are the instruments of the professional and semi-professional commercial bands. The *gralla sec* is without keys; other versions have two or more. With two reeds (only one on a staple) and two pages of measured drawings of reeds. The reeds are totally different from those of other shawms, being spade shaped in profile and carved from *arundo donax* in two separate pieces which are then tied together, rather than being gouged in one piece and folded over and then separated like an oboe or bassoon reed. The staple is brass, quite thick, and sharply conical, hence the very wide reed socket at the top of the instrument. OL 340 mm; ø reed socket 14.5; ø top of bore c. 9; bell ø 50, 53.5 ext; reed L 37; blade L 23.5, W 17.5. Given by the maker. [φ col sl].

XII   146   Shawm, *dultzaina*, Jose Manuel Agirre, Tolosa. Akin to the Navarrese *gaita*, but from the Spanish Basque country. Made of black resin plastic with white (non-ferrous) metal ferrule at each end and between the lowest fingerhole and the 2 lateral vents (ø 10). A chain links the pirouette (pierced with a diamond-shape hole to go over the reed) and the end of the bell-mount, which is saw-toothed and folded in over the end of the bell. Th (ø 7.5) and 7 fingerholes (ø 8.5, 8.5, 8.5, 8, 8, 8, lowest ø 5.5 offset to right). Staple is thick, sharply conical, oval in section, and thickly lapped with cork. Reed is shaped like that of a bagpipe chanter and scraped rather like that of a bassoon, with corner nicks. OL (−14.5 ø 11) 345; ø reed socket 12.8; bell ø 46, 54 ext; reed and staple L 65 (+8), blade L 22.5, W 16. Put together from a stock of prepared parts in the workshop (Ibaiondo 11, 20400 Tolosa, Gipuzkoa) on my order while I watched, with zipped nylon case, and 2 reeds in a reed case. I am grateful to Sabin Bikandi Belandia for introducing me to Agirre, who also makes tambourines, tabors, and side drums to his own design and process, and a *txirula*-like pipe. See *Auzolan* vol. ll/8 (Dec, 19??) And CD, KD 667, and cassette, KT 667, of Agirre and his group, *Tolosako, Dultzaineroak Gaiteroak, 1996.*

XII   94   Shawm, Basque, from the Franco-Spanish border near Irún. Thumb + 7 fingerholes, ø 6.3, th 6.3, 6.3, 7.2, 6.5, 9.2, 6.7, 5.9, the lowest offset for R little finger. Two lateral bell vents ø 9.6. The bell, which has some decorative carving, is less flared than the *dolçaina* and more oboe-like in profile than the *gralla*. Some green paint on the head. No staple or reed. OL (−16 ø 9.0) 335, socket ø 12.5; bell ø 52, 59 ext. Given by Sabin Bikandi Belandia, who had found it in an antique shop, as an exchange for tabor pipe XII 66 when he asked for that back (it has now come back to me because it cracked in use).

IX   34   Shawm, *ciaramella*, Italy. Reamed conical bore. High thumb + 8 fingerholes, ø th 5.9, 4.3, 5.7, five at 5.9, 4.3, + 1 vent on the body ø 5.2, + 2 frontal vents on the bell ø 4.3 and 4.5 probably bored later with a knife. Separate wooden bell on a very coarse screw thread. The high thumbhole, above the uppermost fingerhole, is typical of bagpipe construction. The uppermost vent is on the body above the bell, much as though it were a strongly offset hole for L little finger; the other two are on the bell, facing diagonally forward. All the holes are carved to point slightly downward. OL 335, body L (−12.5 ø 6) 237 (+18.2 ø 14) socket ø 8.5; bell ø 51.5, 74.5 ext. Bought from a stall at an Early Musical Instrument Exhibition at the Horticultural Hall. Jonathan Swayne has kindly provided some suitable reeds. Just as the Breton *bombarde* is used with the bagpipe *biniou*, so the *ciaramella* is used with the bagpipe *zampogna*. [φ col sl]

V   192   Shawm, *tárogató*, József Bige, Budapest. Reamed conical bore. Boxwood with separate bell, the tenon of the body thickly cork lapped. The socket for the staple is bushed with aluminium. High thumb + 7 fingerholes of varying diameter, spacing, and alignment, ø th 6, 5, 6, 6, 7, 5.7, 9.4, 7.2, + 1 dorsal vent ø 6.2. The thumbhole is lined with a metal tube projecting into the bore, like that of a clarinet. An attempt to recreate an extinct instrument. Since it is equipped with an oboe-type reed formed on a very long, narrow, cork-lapped, metal staple, something which is improbable for an early folk instrument, it can be taken to have been an unsuccessful attempt. The sound is much closer to that of an oboe than to that of a shawm and nobody would ever have bothered to ban this as a potentially over-exciting nationalist instrument as the original *tárogató* was banned by the Austrian authorities. Two spare reeds on their staples in a Parker pen refill box. OL 490 mm (not including staple and reed which project 87 mm), body L (−28.1 ø 7.1) 352 (+25 ø 21.7), socket ø 10.8, tapering over 28.1 to step; bell ø 62, 76 ext, bottom of staple ø 7. Bought in a music shop in Amsterdam. [φ 6260/4/40-41].

IX   230   Shawm, *tarompet*, Sunda, West Java. Reamed conical bore. 7 fingerholes all ø 3.8 sloping sharply downwards. Sextuple multiplex reed (3 layers of leaf on each side) as is quite common in South-East Asia (cf the Burmese *hnè*) on a quill staple. Separate wooden top which carries a metal cheek support (traditionally this was of coconut shell) very similar to the *phorbeia* used with the Greek *aulos*, and presumably for the same purpose of supporting the cheeks during circular breathing and avoiding their excessive distension. Separate bell of the same wood decoratively carved with leaf-like patterns. OL, from top of the *phorbeia* to the end of the bell 506; wooden top piece L 41.5 (+9.7 ø 4.8) (fixed at top to *phorbeia*; the end of the quill staple (ø 4.5) fits into it); body L 220 (+16.8 ø 8.7); bell L 160 (upper end of both tapers smoothly) bore L including reed 443, socket ø 3.2, top of body minimum bore 7; bell ø 57.4, ext 71. Bought from Ganesha, a firm run by Marten Timmer, importing material from Indonesia. On loan to the Bate Collection (*x* 2025). [φ col sl]

IX   232   Shawm, *preret*, Lombok, Indonesia. Thumb + 7 fingerholes, all very small, ø c. 3.5. Large flat wooden bell plate, slightly worm damaged, not integral, which pushes on to the tenon of the wooden bell section 142 (+12.9) mm long which has an aluminium ferrule at its upper end. The body is pushed into this upwards from its lower, wider end and is wedged in position with a piece of palm leaf—if the seventh hole is used by players, the body is not in quite far enough at present because the top of the bell section prevents the finger from closing it properly, but it would be risky to force it. A wooden top piece of fixed length (a tenon goes into the socket) fits into the top of the body and a coconut-shell pirouette is held in position on top of it by the short quill staple in the base of the reed. With two reeds of what appears to be palm leaf, held with thread; the reeds are not multiplex. OL without reed c. 482 but including top piece (L 52.7 + 6.8). Top piece bore ø 4 at top, 6 at bottom; socket ø 8.7, tapering to top of bore ø 6, bore ø at bell 30, bell plate ø 160. Bought from Ganesha.

X   280   *Sarune basar* (large sarune), Batak, Sumatra. Shawm with separate bell and bell-flange. Thumb + 5 fingerholes, ø 5.2, th 4.9, 4.9, 5.2, 4.9, 5, thumb + 2 for the upper hand, 3 lower and closer together for the lower. Body slightly torpedo shaped of a dense hardwood with an integral decorative flange projecting back from the head. Bell section a less dense hardwood with a long horn upper ferrule to take the body, and a non-integral bell plate, probably of the same wood, more curved in section than that of IX 232, which fits over a tenon at the bottom of the bell section. A horn top piece fits into the top of the body and is held by a thread (broken and now replaced) to the flange; a coconut-shell pirouette is held in position on the tenon at the top of the top piece by the quill staple of the reed and attached also by thread (also now replaced). The two double reeds are of flattened plant stem similar to the Chinese but slightly larger. OL c. 680 but the top piece only goes about 4 mm into the body and the body only 5mm into the bell, so all is very precarious. Top piece L 57, body L 424, bell L c. 215. Bore ø top of top piece 4.4, tapering to less than 3 (my smallest gauge), bottom of top piece 3.7, top of body 6, tapering to 4.9, bottom of body 10.5, bell 31.5, bell plate 100. Bought from Tim Byard-Jones who kindly brought it back for me.

X   282   *Sarune getep*, the smaller shawm which is used with X 280, is played with a single reed and therefore belongs in 412.212. It is also described here to keep the set together. Thumb + 4 fingerholes, all ø c. 4.9. Similar in shape to the previous. Although this is much shorter than X 280, it is possible that its cylindrical bore allows it to play only an octave above. NB, however, that XI 34 (below) is clearly conical. The body is a different hardwood intermediate between those of X 280, the bell a soft wood with integral bell plate, the coconut-shell pirouette is attached to the flange by a cord. All equally precarious to hold together. OL c. 230, body L 163, bell 68.7, single reed of bamboo (L 72.5) with downcut tongue inserts c. 8 of that length into the top. Bore top ø 6.5 tapering to 5.3, bottom of body 5.7, bell 11.5, bell plate 49. Bought from Tim Byard-Jones who kindly brought it back for me.

XI   32   *Sarune basar*, Samosir Island, Lake Toba, North Sumatra. An instrument of some age, otherwise similar to X 280. Thumb + 5 fingerholes, ø 4.6, th 4.9, 4.9, 4.7, 4.9, 4.9. The body is hardwood with a plain flange at the head projecting backwards; the bell is softwood with a ferrous metal collar instead of horn, the bell plate probably the same wood; both are cruder than X 280; wooden top piece, horn pirouette. The amount of insertion is so slight that it is impossible to hold everything together to get an OL without forcing the insertion and risking cracking. With two reeds of flattened plant stem similar to the Chinese, only one of which has a quill staple. Top piece L 64.5, body L 446, bell L 217. Bore ø top of top piece 4 tapering to less than 3, bottom 4, top of body 6.2, tapering to 4.5, bottom of body 10, bell 37, bell plate 114. Bought in next village to XI 34 by Tony Bingham on my behalf.

XI   34   *Sarune getep*. Because this is played with a single reed, it belongs in 412.212. Again, because both it and XI 32 are used together, it is described here also. All the same wood, similar to that of X 282, but with a non-integral bell plate, coconut-shell pirouette, thumb + 4 burned fingerholes, all ø c. 5.5. OL 227, body L 175, bell 57.5, downcut bamboo single reed 55.7. Bore ø top of body 6.6, tapering to 4.25, bottom of body 7, bell 10, bell plate 56.3.

X   104   Shawm, *pī chawā*, Thailand. Wood with fragments of iridescent shell pressed into the surface. Thumb + 7 fingerholes, all ø c. 4.5. Separate wooden bell similarly decorated, with aluminium upper ferrule. The body is inserted into the bell upwards from the bottom. Quadruplex reed of palm leaf, two each side of windway; coconut-shell pirouette. OL 406, body L 280, bell L 140, socket ø 7.5, top of bore 5.5, bottom of body 13.5, bell 28, ext 69. Bought from Tony Bingham.

According to Dhanit Yupho, there are four separate traditions of shawm in Thailand, the Indian type, the *pī chanai*, the name clearly deriving from Indian *śahnāī*, which is now obsolete; the Burmese type, the *pī mōn*, the name deriving from a Burmese people, the Mon; the Indonesian, or Javanese type, the *pī chawā*; and the indigenous variety, the *pī nai*, with its smaller variants, the *pī klāng* and *pī nōk*. Save that their bells are of different materials, the first three are not greatly dissimilar, though David Morton describes the *pī chanai* as much smaller and shriller than the others. The *pī nai*, however, with its curvilinear form, is entirely distinct and does clearly represent a quite different tradition, and possibly one unrelated to the prevailing Islamic stem. I am fortunate in having examples of most of these types. Morton gives descriptions and detailed photos of the whole process of reed making, and it is probable that this method applies fairly generally to all the South-East Asian multiplex reeds of palm leaf.

VIII   224a   Shawm, *pī mōn*, North Thailand, a tenor shawm. Reamed conical bore, with widely flanged metal bell. 7 fingerholes, the uppermost ø 5.5, the rest 6. Dark-stained wood, which appears to have been worm-eaten before it was turned and varnished, the head wrapped with coloured wool, a strand of which holds the long brass bell, the bottom of the body lapped with string to hold it in the bell. This arrangement derives from the Burmese *hnè*; whether the *hnè* originally had its bell fairly firmly attached in this way, or whether the Thai are a tidier-minded people who prefer not to have the bell flopping as loosely as the Burmese, is perhaps a matter for further research. The bell is made of very thin brass (c. 0.6 thick) which is easily bent between the fingers; as a result the flat flange is never actually flat. The bell is made in three parts, soldered together quite roughly with soft solder: 1) the upper part, c. 110 long, which is very slightly more conical than the body; 2) the lower part, c. 145 long, which is much more sharply conical, the joint between the two being supported by a brass ring soldered over it, and 3) the flat flange 36 wide. Both upper and lower parts have a longitudinal seam overlapping clockwise on the upper part, anti-clockwise on the lower, and also soft soldered; the flange is simply a quoit cut from sheet. Long metal staple wrapped with different wool. No reed or pirouette. OL incl staple 778,680 without, socket ø 11 tapering to top of bore 7.5, bell 115, flange 183.

VIII 224b Shawm, perhaps a different model of *pī chawā* or a small *pī mōn*, North Thailand, a treble shawm. Reamed conical bore, with widely flanged metal bell. 7 fingerholes, all ø c. 6. Similar to the *pī mōn* save that the head is wrapped with green string and that the metal bell is relatively shorter though much the same shape. The upper part of the bell is c. 35 long and lower c. 50, and there is a more prominent ring round the proximal end of the bell. The flange is c. 23 wide and 0.3 thick, but because it is made from a much harder alloy and is slightly saucer shaped, rather than flat, it is considerably stiffer. No reed or pirouette. OL 440, without staple 395, socket ø 9.5 tapering to top of bore 7.3, bell 61.5, flange 107.5. Both bought from Global Village Crafts, South Petherton, where I was told that they were used together.

While much of the stock of Global Village Crafts is tourist tat, they do also buy genuine folk material of all sorts when they see it. While I have some instruments of both varieties, these instruments are in the genuine folk category.

VI   122   Shawm, presumably a *pī klāng*, Bangkok, Thailand. Reamed conical bore. Body with external medial swelling as though pregnant, decorated with many turned and incised rings, but the interior a normal cone—did the bore ever follow the external shape? If not, how did this shape arise? Narrow staple with small quadruplex reed (two layers of leaf on each side), and a spare staple and reed. Six fingerholes, all ø c. 5.2, the four upper distant from the two lower. The distance between the fingerholes, centre to centre, is c. 21 for all save between 4 and 5, where it is 42. There is a turned ring above and below each fingerhole 8.5 apart, so that there is an 8.5 mm "field" for each fingerhole and an empty field between each, with three empty fields between the fourth and fifth. This spacing strongly suggests that this type of shawm may once have had seven fingerholes, as on the preceding instruments. The narrowest parts of the body are immediately above the uppermost fingerhole and immediately below the lowest. OL 340, socket ø 7, top of bore 6, bell 16, top of body external 39, upper waist 30, centre 37.5, lower waist 30 bell 38.5. Bought for me by Ferdinand De Hen, in exchange for a *shofar*. This seems to be the middle of the three sizes; it is intermediate between the sizes that Morton gives for the *pī nōk* and the *pī klāng*. Ferre brought one of the larger, the *pī nai*, for Anthony Baines, and this is now in the Bate Collection (2014). [φ 14/5/40-41; col sl].

I   182   Shawm, *jina* or *haidi*, Inalcy / HONG KONG engraved on the bell and faintly on the wood. Reamed conical bore. Thumb + 7 oval fingerholes, all ø c. 6.5 × 5. Southern Chinese type with wavy outline, a ridge between each fingerhole. The thumb hole is on a ridge (between the thumb- and first fingerhole), whereas the fingerholes are in the valleys between the ridges, as with all the Chinese shawms. Separate brass bell with a medial flange covering the joint between the conical portion and the lower flared portion, the distal end of the latter rolled over outwards to strengthen it. Both sections are longitudinally seamed, both overlapping clockwise. Small size instrument. Staple 82

mm long with pirouette and 2 pierced brass balls, all soldered into place. The body is inserted into the bell from below and is held in the bell with some compound, which I
have not disturbed. OL without staple 299, socket ø 8.4
which is also top of bore, bottom of body 26, bell 99.[φ
1241; b/w slide; reed 3021/2/35].

It has been suggested that the ridges between each fingerhole of the
Chinese shawm can be traced back to the metal rings between each hole of
the Tibetan shawm, or perhaps to a common ancestor. Certainly the complex and ornate staple must derive from or share a common ancestry with
the Tibetan. No other shawms seem to have these features, though Kathleen Schlesinger suggested a connexion between the balls on the Chinese
and Tibetan staple and the *holmos* of the Greek *aulos*.

V   84   Shawm, *suona*, Taiwan, a paper label stuck inside the bell:
Handmade in Taiwan / Republic of China. Reamed conical
bore. Thumb + 7 oval fingerholes, ø 6 × 4, th 6 × 4, 6.2
× 4.5, 6.2 × 4.5, 6.3 × 4.7, 6.7 × 4.7, 6.7 × 5.1, 6.5 × 4.7.
Black wood with very gentle ridges between each fingerhole, the thumbhole on a ridge, Southern Chinese type.
Separate copper bell with brass medial flange covering the
joint, the longitudinal seams overlapping anti-clockwise.
The distal end is rolled over outwards but insufficiently to
strengthen it adequately, for it is somewhat crumpled. Plain
staple without balls, with pirouette rest but no pirouette. A
cheap instrument bought in a Chinese shop in Cleveland,
Ohio in 1970. OL 360, socket ø 8 tapering to top of bore
7.9, bottom of bore 22, bell 130. [φ 6260/8/40-41].

V   190   Shawm, *suona*. Reamed conical bore. Thumb + 7 oval fingerholes, all ø c. 7.5 × 5. Brown wood with ridges between
each fingerhole, the thumbhole on a ridge, Southern Chinese type. Much better quality than the two previous instruments. Separate brass bell with medial flange covering
the joint. Both longitudinal seams overlapped clockwise.
The distal end rolled over outwards for strength. Four Chinese characters cast in the metal of the bell are so worn that
only that at top left can be read: "on the side of a river"
(read by Tau-Tau Liu). Staple 91.5 long with two pierced

brass balls soldered in place; there are traces of where the pirouette rest was fixed. OL without staple 425, socket ø 9.5 tapering to 8.3, bottom of body 27, bell 148. Bought from David Robinson. [φ 6260/4/36-37]

VI　　154　　Shawm, *suona*. Reamed conical bore. Thumb + 7 round fingerholes, ø 6.2, th 6.2, 6.2, 6.4, 6.5, 6.6, 6.6, 7. Black wood with ridges, each decorated with three incised lines, between each fingerhole, the thumbhole on a ridge. The separate brass bell is made in one piece and therefore does not have a medial flange, the Northern Chinese type. There is a very faint trace of a longitudinal hard-soldered meander seam. A paper label has in both Chinese characters and English MADE IN CHINA. Ferrule of brass scrim at the top of the body. The plain staple without balls (L 64.8) has a loose pirouette with holes for attachment cord (replaced). OL without staple 390, socket ø 7.8 with negligible taper, bottom of body 23.5, bell 126. Bought from Raymond Man while his 'shop' was still one small desk in Bill Lewington's instrument shop in Shaftesbury Avenue. [φ 14/5/19-20].

X　　50　　Shawm, *śahnāī*, India. Reamed conical bore. Eight fingerholes, all ø c. 5.5 save for the second, which is 5. Thick wood with separate cast brass bell with four decorative ridges held on with red cloth lapping. The top of the body is slightly reduced, with a very shallow step just above the first fingerhole, suggesting that it may have had a long metal sleeve over it. Long copper staple with quadruplex (2 + 2) palm leaf reed. Clearly the ancestor of, and a much older instrument than, V 48. Well used; all the fingerholes are well worn save the lowest, presumably a vent. OL 428 without staple, staple L 95, including the reed, socket ø 12.5 tapering to top of bore 8, bottom of body 20, bell 79. Bought from Tony Bingham. [φ col sl].

V　　48　　Shawm, *śahnāī*, India. Reamed conical bore. Turned, stained, and varnished wood with a long metal ferrule (white bronze) at the proximal end. The modern *śahnāī* used in classical music today by players such as Bismillah

Khan. Seven fingerholes, all ø c. 4.8. Long staple with large reed of flattened plant stem, and three spares in a wooden holder. Separate decorated metal bell. Mandrel for reed making attached to the staple. Staple L 68.5. OL without staple 427. socket ø 8.5, top of bore 7.5, bottom of body 18, bell 85. Bought for me in Bombay in a market by Professor Ronald Dore. [φ 6260/11/4-5].

V 208 Shawm, *śahnāī*, India. Reamed conical bore. Stained dark wood, highly decorated with carved and painted (pink, yellow, green, mauve) rings. Separate wooden bottle-bell. 8 fingerholes, all ø c. 5.2. Long staple (L 65.2) at present inserts 48.5 into the top, and the thread turk's head at this point suggests that this may be intentional. OL 443 (+ staple and reed), body L 349 (+26.5 ø 17.7), socket ø 9.5 tapering to top of bore 7; bell ø 62, external 71.5. Bought in an Indian shop, Bharneeta, in Hampstead Road. [φ 6260/4/38-39].

I 190 Shawm, *śahnāī*, India. Reamed conical bore. A long instrument, possibly a South Indian *nāgasvaram*. Seven fingerholes, the two uppermost ø 5, the rest 5.5, + 5 vents, 1 frontal ø 6 and 2 on each side ø 5.5. Separate metal bell missing (that from I 178 fits). Body L 484 (+20.5 ø 23.3), socket ø 8.5, top of bore 7.5. Bought from Page Phillips, Kensington Church Street. [φ 1234/E/27-28; b/w slide].

I 184 Shawm, *śahnāī*, India, probably from the Calcutta area (located by comparison with one labelled Calcutta which was acquired by A. C. Baines and is now in the Bate Collection, *x 289*). Reamed narrow conical bore with a deep well for the staple. Straight exterior with integral bottle bell. Thumb + 7 fingerholes all ø c. 5.5. Long narrow brass staple (L 84), wooden pirouette. Body L (−44.5 ø 7) 337, socket ø 11.5 tapering to step at top of bore, top of bell ø 15.5, bell 65, 70 ext. [φ 1241 and 1284/2].

I 178 Drone shawm, *śruti*, India. Reamed conical bore. Two rough-cut holes ø 4.5 and 5.5 low down which can be stopped with wax to vary the drone pitch + 2 lateral drilled vents ø 5.7 immediately above a heavy turned baluster. The proximal end also has heavy decorative turning. Separate heavy cast gold-painted brass bell which also fits I 190. OL 665, body L 596 (+30 ø 25), socket ø 11.5 tapering to top of bore 7.7, bottom of body internally pentagonal, bell ø 85.7, 92 ext. Bought from Page Phillips. [φ 1234/E/25-26].

The drone is an essential feature of Indian music, giving a continual pitch referent, with the result that tuning is far more precise than in Western music—ask anyone to sing a scale slowly, first alone and then referring each pitch to a tonic drone, and the second is always better in tune even for the "non-harmonic" (non-common chord) pitches. In addition, as Nazir Jairazbhoy has pointed out in his book on *Rāga*, the drone creates tension, for the nearer music gets to a consonance, the more dissonant it becomes, and it is dissonances that keep music moving, because consonances are positions of rest whereas dissonances are always seeking resolution.

VIII   208   Wind-cap shawm, India. Reamed conical bore. High thumb + 7 fingerholes, ø th 5.1, 5.1, 5.7, 6.6, 7, 7.9, 7.9, 8.2 + 2 lateral vents 8.8 and 9.2. The bell is a separate piece of wood glued over the end of the body. Windcap is of different wood. Probably a modern development, a conflation of the *śahnāī* and the Highland bagpipe practice chanter which has a similar windcap and fingerhole distribution and sizing. The Scottish Highland bagpipe is now widely used in India, to the extent that it has displaced most of the indigenous types. With a little retuning of the fingerholes, these instruments have proved popular with early music groups in Britain as treble windcap shawms. OL 525, L without windcap or reed 415, socket ø 6.8 tapering to top of bore ø 4.3, bottom of body ø 22.5, bell 59, 69.4 ext. Bought from Raymond Man, Neal Street, Covent Garden.

V   188   Shawm, *horanāva*, Sri Lanka. Reamed conical bore. Seven finger holes ø 4.6, 5.3, 5.5, 6, 5.7, 5.7, 5.3. Black painted wood with yellow painted rings between each fingerhole, slightly warped front to back. Separate brass bell. A metal ring on a loose ferrule round the top of the body and another on the bell suggests that there may once have been a chain linking the two. The brass staple is immovable without using undue force. The *horanāva* is much smaller than the Indian *śahnāī* but is clearly closely related to it. OL 269, body L(+ staple 33) 170 (+12ˑø 18.5); bell ø 67, 74 ext. Bought from David Robinson. [φ 6260/11/8-9].

II 124a/b Pair of shawms, *rgya-gling*, Tibet. Thumb + 7 heavily worn fingerholes, (a) the highest ø 6, all the others 7; (b) 5.7, th 6.2, 6.5, 6.5, 7.4, 7.1, 7, 6.8. A brass ring set with alternately a coral or a turquoise (the second stone, presumably a turquoise, is missing) between each fingerhole. Cast brass ornamental ferrule round the head. Large separate brass bells, with cast brass and copper decoration similar to that of the long Tibetan trumpets. The leading melodic instruments of the temple orchestras. Mireille Helffer gives very full details of these instruments. Nineteenth-century examples now lacking their ornate staples and pirouettes. The bells of both are badly brass-rotted, and that of (a) was cleaned and experimentally protectively waxed by Harris Plating of Kings Cross. The bells are made in one piece with an almost imperceptible longitudinal hard-soldered meander joint. The elaborate medial cast copper flange is purely decorative, though it would seem to be ancestral to the functional Chinese medial flange; perhaps Tibetan bells were also once made in two sections, upper and lower. The bodies are luted into the bells with wax over about 50 or so mm. (a) OL 535, bell L 220, socket ø 14.5, top of bore 11.3, bottom of body 29, bell 145 × 165. (b) has the same decoration but the copper on the bell is badly rotted and the top two jewels are missing. OL 535, bell L 220, socket ø 13.5, top of bore 11.3, bottom of body 39, bell 150 × 160. Bought from Paxman, the french horn makers, before they moved to Long Acre from Gerrard Street, where these, and some other instruments which I also bought, hung on the wall; why a French horn specialist should have a set of Tibetan shawms is a puzzle, but possibly the staples always were missing and Paxman therefore thought that a trumpet-type mouthpiece was used. [φ 1234/A/12 of both; b/w slide of the cleaned one].

II   124c   Shawm, *rgya-gling*, Tibet. One of a pair similar to a and b
                  but in markedly better condition though with the same parts
                  missing. Also missing are a turquoise and two corals. The
                  order of jewels is reversed. The fingerholes are worn, but
                  perceptibly less so, ø 5.7, th 7, 5.7, 6.5, 6.5, 6.8, 6, 6. A chain
                  joins the top ferrule to the bell. If the bell was held on with
                  wax, this is now missing. The cast medial copper flange is
                  slightly less massive. OL 54, bell L 228, socket ø 13, top of
                  bore 11.2, bottom of body too far up to measure accurately
                  but c. 28, bell c. 160. Same source. [φ 1234/A/13].

IX   28   Shawm, *rgya-gling*, Tibet. Thumb + 7 fingerholes, ø 5.7, th
                  4.5, 6, 6.2, 6, 6.3, 6.7, 6. A rather more recent example of
                  this instrument and in much better condition, complete in-
                  cluding the staple with two large pierced brass balls and or-
                  nate pirouette, save that all the jewels, which were larger,
                  are missing from the rings between the fingerholes. The
                  balls, the pirouette, and the bottom plate are all loose on
                  the staple, unlike those of Chinese shawms, which presum-
                  ably were also loose in earlier times. The staple is chained
                  to a brass ferrule round the top of the instrument, and that
                  to two points on the bell. Silvered bell with brass decora-
                  tion including a third ring at the distal end, which is rolled
                  over the end inward. The second ring from the top is
                  pierced for the thumbhole, unlike the three previous
                  shawms, which manage to fit both the thumbhole and the
                  next fingerhole between two rings. OL including the staple
                  590—the staple projects 112.5, so presumably about this
                  length is missing from the above three shawms—bell L 170,
                  socket ø 11, top of bore 8.6, bottom of body too far up to
                  measure accurately but c. 25, bell c. 142. Bought from Tony
                  Bingham. [φ col sl].

X   52   Shawm, perhaps Tibet. Thumb + 7 fingerholes, ø 6, th 4,
                  6, 5.5, 7, 6, 6, 6. Body only. There is a metal ring between
                  each fingerhole but no jewels or sockets for them. The up-
                  permost ring is pierced for the thumbhole, with a metal
                  tube projecting into the bore (there is not, and never was, a
                  ring above the top fingerhole whereas there is on all four

previous shawms). There is a metal ferrule round the head; the bottom of the body is marked where it was held in the bell. The wood is paler than that of the Tibetan instruments and less than 1.5 mm thick. The lowest fingerhole is offset for the R little finger but was originally in line with the others—the original hole is neatly plugged with a wooden plug which slightly projects into the bore. OL 339, socket ø 12 tapering to 11.8, bottom of body 30.5, and clearly knife scraped. One of a batch of shawms bought from Tony Bingham just as he had bought them.

X   56   Shawm, Newar, Nepal. Apparently deriving from the Tibetan *rgya-gling* but made by splitting, gouging, and reuniting the wood, the seam waxed at the proximal end, above the finger- and thumbholes; presumably insertion of the staple had spread it. Curved in a C-shape, with fingerholes on the concave side. Plaited bands of leather between the fingerholes instead of metal rings. High thumb (above the highest ring) + 8 fingerholes, five highest ø 7, then 6.5, 6.5, 6, 6, very well worn except for the lowest hole, which was presumably a vent. Staple missing, brass bell, with two decorative rings, of lighter metal and much smaller than the Tibetan, longitudinally seamed with a meander joint. OL 455, bore length c. 460, socket ø 11.5 × 12 tapering to top of bore c. 8, bottom of body 20, bell 85, 103 × 109 ext. Bought from Tony Bingham. Laurent Aubert confirms the attribution with much further detail. [φ col sl].

X   54   Shawm, *hnè-galei*, Burma, the smaller of the two sizes. Reamed conical red-painted wooden body with loose brass bell held on only by a cord (missing but replaced). The bell has a medial flange soldered on over the joint (like the Chinese) and a fine soldered longitudinal meander joint. Thumb + 7 fingerholes all c. 5.5. With octuplex reed (4 + 4) of toddy palm leaf with very short staple. Body L 267, bell L 128, OL what you will, since the bell is not fixed, socket ø 8.5 tapering to top of bore 7, bottom of body 19, bell now c. 90, c. 100 ext, but badly distorted. Bought from Tony Bingham.

The loose bell of the *hnè*, which just flops around, held only by its cord, is something of a mystery; it seems to relate to no other shawm, and one wonders whether by any chance it was a feature added, by parallel with the Indian instrument, to an otherwise indigenous wooden instrument (but see the comment to VIII 224a above). John Okell's field recordings (copies of some of which he gave me) are evidence that the multiplex reed, which he said was soaked in green tea for half an hour or so before use, and one of which he gave me, is no hindrance to a fluent technique and a wide range, for some of his recordings are of non-stop playing (i.e., with circular breathing) over a two-octave compass for an hour or more.

BAGPIPES WITH
DOUBLE REED—422.112/.21-62 OR .22-62

The earliest evidence for the bagpipe cited by Anthony Baines (*Bagpipes*, pp. 63–64) is a rather uncertain reference of about 400 B.C., from Aristophanes in *The Acharnians*, which could as easily refer to a bladder pipe. There is a much more positive one a few centuries later, in the second century A.D., from Suetonius's *Life of Nero*, followed by Dio Chrysostom who said that Nero played "the *aulos* with the armpit, a bag being thrown under it, in order that he might escape the disfigurement." The Greek *aulos*, like all the instruments so far described here, was blown with circular breathing, by breathing in through the nose while blowing out from the cheeks, so that there was no cessation of sound. A clear indicator of this is the use of the *phorbeia*, a strap of cloth or leather which supported the cheeks and, by reducing the strain on the muscles which run across them, prevented excessive distension, which would lead to the disfigurement Dio referred to; Nigerian *algaita* players, whose cheeks are distended like balloons while playing, wind up after a few years with dewlaps like a bloodhound, because the cheeks, when distended too much and for too long, lose their elasticity and fail to return to their original shape.

The knack of circular breathing is not difficult to acquire; it is taught to children with a straw and a glass of water; they practise until they can keep the bubbles incessantly flowing. It is much more difficult to equalise the air pressure so that when changing from diaphragm breathing to cheek breathing, whose muscles are normally much weaker than those of the diaphragm, there is no drop in air pressure, which would result in a flattening of pitch. Ethnographic recordings of children producing a continuous sound without effort, but with a pitch change with each switch of breathing method, are evidence that this is where the difficulty lies. The use of an external reservoir, such as a bag, obviates this problem and, because it does not require the distension of the cheeks, could have been attractive to the ancient Greeks, with their emphasis on bodily perfection, and certainly to Nero with his well-known personal vanity. An incidental advantage is that a bagpipe allows a player to sing to his own accompaniment, provided that he keeps the phrases short enough that the bag is not exhausted before he stops singing and can refill it; this technique can be heard today in many areas.

The earliest iconographic evidence found so far (all post-Roman; Canon Galpin's Roman carving from Richborough—*Old English Instruments* fig. 33—is now known to be a mediæval knife handle) is the illustrations of the *Cántigas de Santa Maria* (Escorial ms b.I.2—about 1280), where a number of well-developed bagpipes of several different types are shown, indicating that the bagpipe was by no means new in Spain at that date. Other illustrations, including many church carvings, can be found all over Europe within the next fifty years. However, the instrument in the well-known illustration from the York Psalter (Glasgow UL, Hunterian 229, f. 21v) of about 1175 (plate 8 in my *Medieval & Renaissance*), which Armstrong Davison claimed was a Northumbrian bagpipe, does not appear to be a bagpipe of any sort.

Obviously another advantage of the bag is that it can carry more than one pipe. It would seem, however, that, although most of the pipes shown in the *Cántigas* have drones, some with more than one, most early mediæval instruments were without any drone, and the later ones had only a single drone. The date of the adoption of a second drone in Scotland, and then a third, is not clear, but the first tenor drone may not be earlier than the eighteenth century, with the nineteenth century more likely for the second. Only in the last century and more recently has the Highland pipe achieved its present world-wide dominance and there are still many other types of bagpipe in existence.

On those bagpipes which have a conical shawm chanter, the use of a double reed on the chanter and single reeds on cylindrical drones is normal. The Italian *zampogna* of the Abruzzi is one of the few pipes with conical drones and all double reeds; the seventeenth- and eighteenth-century

French *musette du cour* also used double reeds throughout (see Mersenne's illustration), even though the drones were cylindrical. Bagpipes with cylindrical chanters normally, though not invariably (see IX 26 here), use single reeds on both the chanter and the drone.

III   226   Bagpipe, *gaita gallega*, Spain. A small-size example. Conical bore boxwood chanter with double reed, high thumb + 7 fingerholes, the lowest offset for R little finger, th 2.8, 3.1, 3.6, 4.2, 5.2, 6.2, 6.4, 5.2 + 2 lateral vents 5.5 and 6.2. Single cylindrical boxwood drone with single reed. Bag of old motor inner tube as is usual today, which has now perished and cracked, covered with red cloth, rather torn. Drone in 3 sections (plus stock). The mediæval type of single-drone bagpipe, still used in Spain. Brought back and given by my mother; one extra of each reed brought by Ottily Pannett. Mouthpipe L 90.6 (+16), leather non-return valve held by thread lapping. Chanter L (+20.7 ø 3.9) 228, socket ø 6.5 tapering to top of bore; bell ø 18.5, ext 35.6, drone bore ø 9, with bottle bell, aperture ø 13, ext ø 48, L (+19.3) 455 + stock, drone tenons each 46 long for tuning. [φ 1234/O/2-4; b/w slide]

II   216   Bagpipe, Highland Great Pipes, *piob mhór*, P. HENDERSON/ GLASGOW, early twentieth century. Conical rosewood chanter, painted to look like ebony, with double reed, high thumb + 7 fingerholes in a straight line, th 4.8, 5.1, 5.9, 7, 7.3, 8.1, 8.4, 8.5 + 2 lateral vents 9 and 9.2. Two tenor drones in 2 sections. The lower section of the second drone is a replacement, with ivory mounts differing in profile from the rest as well as material, and its stock has a metal ferrule, presumably covering some damage. One bass drone in 3 sections, all similar wood. All the drones are cylindrical with single reeds. Imitation ivory mounts (probably celluloid), tartan cover to bag. The non-return valve on the mouthpipe (a leather flap) did not function so a black plastic Alexander patent mouthpipe, with a ball non-return valve, was bought from George Alexander, a bagpipe specialist in an attic in Gerrard Street, Soho, to replace the original yellow plastic mouthpipe. Bought from Payton,

Camden Passage. Chanter L (+25.4 ø 4.2) 337, socket ø 7 tapering to top of bore, bell ø 22.3, sole plate ø 75.0; first tenor drone bore ø 7.5, aperture 14.2, L (+28.5) 375; second tenor bore ø 8.3, same aperture; bass drone bore ø 7.5 at top of lowest section, 8.8 at top of middle, 15 aperture, L (+28.9) 805. [φ 1234/P/17-19; b/w sl].

VIII 204   Bagpipe, Highland Great Pipes, chanter only. Presumably Pakistan (the Highland pipes are widely used on the Indian sub-continent) since it was from the World of Islam Exhibition. Th 4.7, 4.7, 5.7, 6.6, 7.1, 7.8, 8, 8.2, + vents 9 and 9.8. Cast aluminium sole plate. Bought at Sotheby's after the sale 5/11/81, lot 55, which had attracted no bid. L (+26.2 ø 5.75) 335, socket ø 6.5 tapering to top of bore, bell ø c. 22 (somewhat haggled by knife), sole plate ø 63.3.

IX 26   Bagpipe, *duda*, Anatoly Zajaruzny, Ukraine. Chanter marked cursive KNEB—1982 by hot iron and hot iron decoration round fingerholes. Judging from the descriptions of the Ukrainian *duda* in the Vertkov *Atlas*, this is a somewhat hypothetical reconstruction of the Eastern Ukrainian bagpipe. It was made as a gift for me. There appears to be some influence from the Spanish *gaita gallega*. Goat-head chanter, cylindrical bore with a plastic double reed on a thin brass staple, with a white cowhorn bell and thumb ø 4.2 + 7 fingerholes ø 2.5, 2.8, 2.8, 3.2, 2.5, 4, 3.5 (offset to R). Single drone with 2 vents, both plugged with wooden plugs (held on with thread), also with a plastic double reed inside the bag (!), similar to that of the chanter, also with a horn bell. Both bells have dentated ends and some dentations are bent and others broken off due to my clumsiness—they are very fragile. Drone reed marked 1 in pencil, chanter reed marked 2. Green felt cover to bag, tasselled cord like that of the *gaita gallega* pendant from the drone. Blackhorn mouthpiece with leather non-return valve. Chanter L (+12 ø c. 3.6) 160 (+ glued into horn), horn L c. 13; socket cork lined ø c. 5, drone bore 5. On loan to the Bate Collection (*x 4086*).

OBOES

The oboe was devised in the mid-seventeenth century, perhaps at the French Court by members of the Hotteterre family and their associates. If this were so, its invention was probably in response to Louis XIV's desire to dance more comfortably indoors in the *Ballets du Cour*, for dancing outdoors would have been unpleasant in winter. The loudness of the shawm, then the most important of the orchestral woodwind instruments, was intolerable indoors and something quieter would have been needed. However, there are also strong possibilities of a Dutch origin, perhaps by Richard Haka and his contemporaries or predecessors. Josef Marx postulated 1660 for the first intimations for the oboe; 1650 or even 1640 have been mooted more recently, and dates earlier still keep appearing. Certainly there seems no doubt that the oboe is earlier than the *Duytse Schalmey* which was, at one time, considered to be its precursor but was more recently recognised to be a "new shawm," created in the later seventeenth century because the oboe was not loud enough for military use. However in the recently published *Catalogue of Double Reed Instruments, Collection Gemeentemuseum* (p. 50), it is stated that the Duytse Schalmey has "a soft tone, certainly no louder than that of the baroque oboe." If this were correct, and if they were using the right sort of reed (and who can ever say anything certain about that!), it would leave us once again with no idea about the origin or purpose of the Schalmey.

The bore of the oboe is more slender than that of the shawm, and the reed was longer, narrower (though by no means as long and narrow as today's reed), made of thinner and more delicate cane with a different scrape, and fully controlled by the player's lips. Thus the player had much more control over tuning by adjusting the pressure of his lips on the reed than he had had on the shawm and, because he did not have to blow hard enough to force closed a well-opened, heavy double reed as on the shawm, he could now play as softly as he pleased. At the same time, the control of his lips on the reed helped overblowing to the upper register, thus increasing the range.

So far as we know (nobody can produce an instrument saying "this is the first of all oboes," but see Bruce Haynes on this point), the oboe had, from its first invention, the open-standing great key to extend the range to middle C. It also had, like the transverse flute, a key for the chromatic note immediately above the "six-finger note," that produced by closing all six fingerholes. As on the transverse flute, the six-finger note was D, but unlike the flautists, who called theirs the D♯ key, oboists called it the E♭ key, an indication of the tonalities in which the two instruments were happiest—flautists liked sharp keys and oboists preferred flat ones. Also unlike the transverse flute, this E♭ key had to be duplicated to make it accessible to either little finger. Players had not, in the seventeenth century, settled on left hand above right, as we play today, and whereas the foot joint of the transverse flute could be turned to bring the key under either hand, the keys on the oboe were above the joint between the lower body and the bell. Thus there was no way to turn an E♭ key to meet the hand, and duplication was the only recourse. The great key had a forked touch so that it could be reached by either little finger.

Other chromatic notes were played by cross-fingering, by covering holes below the lowest open fingerhole. The natural scale was that of D major and, putting things very simply, opening each fingerhole in turn from the bottom produced the scale of that key. Opening the lowest hole produced E, opening the lowest two holes produced F sharp. To obtain an F ♮, the lowest hole was covered again, leaving the second open, while very slightly relaxing the pressure on the reed. The other notes foreign to a D major scale were similarly obtained. The only chromatic note which cannot be produced by cross-fingering is that immediately above the six-finger note; hence the need for the E♭ key. The lack of provision for the low C ♯ is confirmation that the great key was an extension rather than an integral part of the range.

Cross-fingered notes are never quite as clear in sound as those produced without closing lower holes, and they are particularly difficult to play in the rapid reiterations known then as shakes, and now as trills. As a result, additional, key-covered holes were eventually provided which, when opened, produced the pitches foreign to D major. These came later on the oboe than on the transverse flute both because the oboe suffered much less, due to the small diameter of its fingerholes, from the problems of poor venting which result from closing holes when cross-fingering, and because control of the reed made it rather easier to help cross-fingering into tune. Thus while the transverse flute had these extra keys certainly by the 1780s, they only appeared on the oboe in the first decade of the nineteenth century and only became at all common in the second decade and later.

Two-key oboes (the duplicate E♭ key disappeared around 1750, though the C key retained its forked touch for left and right little-finger well into the nineteenth century, presumably for the sake of appearance) were still being used by professional oboists long after the one-key transverse flute vanished from all but the most amateur or military circles.

Keys are either closed-standing or open-standing. Open-standing keys are normally used to close holes which are beyond the reach of the fingers, such as the lowest hole on the oboe. Closed-standing keys cover the extra holes, usually for chromatic notes, which are outside the natural scale of the instrument. In both cases, the keys are named for the note produced by operating them, by closing an open key or opening a closed key (see the diagrams here of bassoons with holes and keys identified, and of Triébert's système 3 and other later, and more complex oboe systems, which have been drawn by Tetsu Ito, a young Japanese oboe maker, who measured all my oboes, and many others, while he was studying at the London Guildhall University). Keys specially provided for trills are called trill or shake keys, and those used to produce the upper range of the instrument or to steady certain notes or improve their tuning, are called speaker, harmonic, or vent keys respectively. Some keys are used for two or more of these purposes, and it is very probable that ensuring good trills was the initial purpose of most closed keys.

Naming fingerholes is more controversial because some authorities use the name of the note produced by closing a hole, whereas others prefer to use the name of the note produced by opening that hole. The latter method is preferable, and is used here, because the name is then that of the note which speaks through that hole. The oboe sounds D with all finger-closed holes covered (the six-finger note); uncovering the lowest hole produces E, so that hole is called the E hole. The next hole is the F♯, and so on up.

Unfortunately, this collection, unlike the Bate Collection, cannot show a full sequence of early oboes, illustrating the gradual addition of these keys, but their gradual increase in number is parallelled on the amateur's oboe, the *musette*. The *musette* originated perhaps as a French pastoral oboe (presumably a shawm, such as the Breton bombarde) or perhaps as a mouth-blown derivant of the chanter of the bagpipe of the same name. In either case, it was modified and refined by late nineteenth-century instrument makers into an amateur's oboe, which became popular, perhaps analogously with the flageolet, though because of the fragility of its double reed no type of oboe has ever been as popular as any variety of the flute or even the clarinet. Very few of these late nineteenth-century instruments ever have a maker's name. By this date, of course, players were universally playing with left hand over the right, and therefore there is only one E♭ key. As an amateur's instrument it was presumably thought unnecessary to have the extension to written middle C—with instruments of smaller or larger size than the standard, one normally refers to keys by the same names as on the standard size. The bell has normally a bulbous profile externally although internally it is a simple cone, perhaps for greater strength and certainly for increased volume, for the added mass inhibits the vibration of the wood, leaving more energy free to come out as sound.

I   176b/c   Two *musettes*, anon. Brown wood. One key (E♭). (b) is on loan to the Bate Collection *(x 2003)*. Thumb ø 3.5 + 7 fingerholes ø 3.5, 5.2, 5.5, 5.5, 6.2, 4.3 // 3.5 (a small hole by the key touch), + 2 vents ø 5.5. Bulb bell. OL 354, socket ø 8.8, top of bore ø 4.7, body L 214 (+16.8 ø 11), bell (−7.5) 430, ø 26, ext 36. I 176c could not be found when compiling this catalogue. [φ 1234/G/23 and 1234/I/30; b/w slide, col sl].

I   176a   *Musette*, anon. Blackwood, mount or ferrule, presumably white bronze, missing from the top of each joint. Six white bronze keys, E♭ on the bell, cross F, A♭, B♭, upper C♮, rear speaker (keys were not removed to measure the holes below them, but this can always be done if it were thought to be useful). High thumb ø 3.3 + 6 fingerholes ø 3.4, 4.3, 4.2, 4, 5.6, 4.7 + 2 lateral bell vents ø 6 and 6.5. Bulb bell. OL 359, body L (−11.3 ø 4.6) 217 (+16.3 ø 9.7), reed socket ø 6.7, cylindrical to step at top of bore; bell ø 24.7, ext 36.9. [φ1284/2/12].

The term "white bronze" is used here, following Philip Bate's example, because of the difficulty of distinguishing between German silver, nickel silver, maillechort, and other alloys of similar constituents and different patent names; all are based on copper with the addition of nickel and other minerals.

I   176d   *Musette*, anon. Dark brown wood, perhaps African blackwood, 2 white bronze mounts. 6 keys of the same material, E♭, cross F, A♭, B♭, upper C♮, and a rear speaker. Thumb ø

3 + 7 fingerholes ø 3.5, 4.3, 3.5, 3.2, 4.8, 4.8, // 3.8 just above the key touch. Rather better quality instrument. Slender bulb bell. OL 358, socket ø 6.2, top of bore 4.5, body L 221(+14.8 ø 9.2), bell L (−15.1) 140 ø 25.5, ext 32. Given by Mrs. I. Hodson. On loan to the Bate Collection (*x 2004*). [φ 1234/J/26-27].

VII   152   *Musette*, anon. Rosewood and 3 white bronze mounts. 6 keys, E♭, both side and cross F, A♭, B♭, upper C♮. Thumb ø 2.8 + 6 fingerholes ø 2.9, 4.7, 4.8, 3.4, 3.4, 4.7. Vents ø 5.6. Bulb bell. OL 352, socket ø 7.8, top of bore 4.8, body L 221 (+15.5 ø 8.8), bell L (−15.8) 132 ø 23.7, ext 37.8. Dorothy Crump Memorial Gift, given by her daughter Heather. On loan to the Bate Collection (*x 2002*). [φ 1249].

III   148   *Musette*, anon. Brown wood. 6 white bronze keys, E♭, long and cross F, A♭, B♭, upper C♮, and mount at the top of the bell joint. High thumb ø 3 + 6 fingerholes ø 3.5, 4.2, 5.7, 3.2, 4.7, 4.2, + 2 bell vents 5.5 and 5.8, with an extra vent or seventh hole ø 3.3 hand drilled below the touch of the E♭ key on the bell. Flared bell. A previous owner has opened the top to try to make a descant cornett and has crudely chipped away some of the top ring of the body to reduce the embouchure rim thickness, without trying to smooth it into a circle. OL 371, body L (−12.5 ø 3.8) 225 (+15.2 ø 10.2), ø top of socket now c. 12 (exterior 17-17.5), original ø c. 7, cylindrical to step at top of bore; bell ø c. 35, ext 51.4. Bought from Joan Rimmer. [φ 1234/B/12-13].

IV   112   *Musette, marked:* FABRIK / MARKE / [lyre] / TRADE / MARK / GHS (the S largest), which according to *NLI* is the mark of G. H. Hüller, working in Hermesgrün 1878–83, and Schöneck 1883–modern; I presume that the S stands for Schöneck and that the date is therefore post-1883. 6 white bronze keys and bell and socket mounts, E♭, long and cross F, A♭, B♭, upper C♮. Thumb ø 2.9 + 6 fingerholes ø 4.1, 4.4, 4.4, 4.4, 4.9, 4.2, vent 4.4 (LH only). Bell of Austrian oboe pattern with a raised ring just below the vent, lighter wood than the body and the rim slightly chipped, and slightly fancy head. OL 360, socket ø 6.8, 16.3 to step at top of bore, body L (−16.5 ø 4.5) 225 (+16.9 ø 10.2), bell L 135 ø 27.7, rim ext 43.2. Bought from Webster. On loan to the Bate Collection *(x 2005)*. [φ 1234/B/14-15; all four Bate Loan on col sl].

I 188 Oboe, William Milhouse, London, c. 1800–20, *marked:* MILHOUSE / LONDON. Boxwood, bulb top, unmounted, 2 silver keys with round heads in rings, the C key with forked touch (the spring now soldered to the key, originally SATK), neither key visibly marked. Fingerhole ø 3.3, 3.3, 2.5 + 2.5 // L3.1 + R3.5, 5.5, 4.2 (keys were not removed) + 2 bell vents 5.5. Cecil Adkins type 6a. The undercut bell is fished with heavy thread to strengthen cracks which had been glued. OL 572; reed socket ø 7.6, conical to step at top of bore; upper joint L (−18.2 ø 4.8) 213 (+21.5 ø 9.5), lower joint L (−21.5) 212 (+27 ø 14.5), bell L (−27) 145 ø 39.3, widest 43.5, external 60.8. Bought from John Sothcott who had bought it from Eric Halfpenny, who illustrated it in *GSJ* 2 with an X-radiograph, the original of which he passed on to me before he died. Illustrated also in my *Romantic & Modern Instruments* pl. X. Edinburgh Galpin Society Exhibition, 1968, no. 86, *PTY* no 1. Copies are available of a drawing with detailed measurements by Tetsu Ito. [φ 1256/4/5; 120/1; 120/3;b/w slides].

IV 204 Oboe, *marked:* [monogram] / GAUTROT-MARQUET / Breveté S.G.D.G / PARIS / 1103, post 1875. To B♮. Rosewood, white bronze keys and bell ring. Twelve keys, including long and cross upper C♮, and brille to close F♯ vent. The French oboe before Triébert's système 3, with only one octave key and no connexion between the R little finger keys and the brille and cross F♯. Half-hole key end-mounted with pin for touch, 1 speaker. 2 long levers for L little finger for alternative E♭ and low B♮. From hole 2: ø 3.5, 2.4 + 2.4 (L higher than R) // 3.9, 5, 5. Sockets metal lined. Undercut bell. OL 563, reed socket ø 7, cylindrical to step at top of bore; upper joint L (−17.9 ø 4.7) 211.2 (+19.9 ø 10.3), lower joint L (−19.9) 206.5 (+25.7 ø 15.0), bell L (−26.9) 143.8 ø 38, widest 44.3, ext

55.8. From Philip Bate in exchange for an Evette & Schaeffer soprano saxophone in alto shape (IV 128, now his
loan to the Bate Collection *x 50*); with round label 45 D,
and 8468 on label inside bell. Copies are available of a
drawing with detailed measurements by Tetsu Ito. [φ
1234/O/32-34; b/w slide].

The range of the oboe was extended from the middle of the nineteenth century by adding a key to cover one of the bell vents, closing which
produced B♮. A second key was added later to extend the range further to
B♭, now the normal lowest note.

V   232   Oboe, *marked:* BREVETE / [castle with 3 merlons] /
TRIÉBERT / A PARIS, c. 1860. Probably rosewood, white
bronze keys, mounts and bell ring. Système 3 to B♭. 13 keys
+ brille to close F♯ vent (one key—the cross F natural—is
missing, the hole plugged with cork), frontal music holder
socket on the bell. Figure-8 shape half-hole key, 2 octave
keys, long levers for L little finger for low B and B♭ on the
bell. From hole 2 ø 3.7, 2.4 + 2.4 (L is higher then R) //
4.7, 5.2, 4.7. No undercutting on the bell. Cork-lapped
tenons. Hole 3 double. OL 580, reed socket ø 7.25, cylindrical to step at top of bore; upper joint L (−17.6 ø 4.94)
224.7 (+18.6 ø 10), lower joint L (−18.8) 193.7 (+18.5 ø
14.5), bell L (−18.6) 160 ø 39.3, ext 52. Illustrated in my
Romantic & Modern Instruments pl. XI, *PTY* no. 33. Bought
from Stirling Antiques, Abinger Hammer. Copies are available of a drawing with detailed measurements by Tetsu Ito.
[φ 6260/4/33-35; 120/2].

Guillaume and Frédéric Triébert, father and son, established the
modern oboe, working through one system after another in Paris from
about 1840 onwards. There is still argument regarding the meaning of
the castle and the significance of the number of its merlons or crenella-
tions, which are sometimes three and sometimes four, but according to
William Waterhouse and Phillip T. Young this mark, with Breveté and
three merlons, is that of Frédéric. The firm of Triébert was eventually
bought by Gautrot, and their systems were further developed, culminat-
ing in the Conservatoire system, by their ex-foreman, François Lorée,
who established his own firm and also adapted the Boehm system to the

oboe.

VII   228   Oboe, J.T.L. on thumb hook, mark used by Jérôme Thibouville Lamy, France, post-1866 *(NLI)*. Rosewood and white bronze. To B♭. Boehm system with thumb plate, 5 rings, butterfly-style key, alternative E♭ one way, B♭ the other, 2 octave keys. From hole 2 ø 4.5, 5.6, 7.1, 6, 7.2. The top is fished in two places with coarse thread, presumably covering a crack (and perhaps a mark). OL 527, reed socket ø 7.0, cylindrical to step at top of bore; one-piece body L (−18.7 ø 5.15) 463 (+13.6 ø 19.9), bell L (−14) 79 ø 36.3, ext 49.0. Bought from Tony Bingham with the proceeds of extra fees for the film *Dragonslayer*. [φ 1251/25-27].

Boehm's system has never really suited the oboe because the wider tone holes produce too coarse a sound; however, for that very reason it has been popular for military bands. One compromise which is sometimes found is a Boehm lower (right-hand) joint with a normal upper joint. There is an essential distinction between Boehm's system, the acoustic perfection of bore and relative fingerhole diameters, as here, and his mechanism, which made the adoption of the system possible, and which has been used, more or less modified, on all woodwind instruments since his day, especially of course on the clarinet which has adopted his name.

Some instruments were provided as props for *Dragonslayer* (leading to the breakage of a fiddle bow and the resolution never again to lend for props for either screen or stage) and the extra fees bought a number of inexpensive instruments of no great quality or interest but useful as examples of types not otherwise represented in the collection.

VII   230   Oboe, CASTEGNIER / ET / MICOLLIER / A / PARIS, c. 1875. To low A with 5 open standing keys at the foot, presumably for C♯, C, B, B♭, A. Complex system with Barret action and automatic octaves, perhaps that which, according to Constant Pierre (p. 322), won these makers a prize in 1878. Triple butterfly key plus a separate touch for the upper little finger, rings for both hands. Each key is controlled by a grub screw as are all the clutches and linkages. Fingerhole ø 4.7, 4.2 // 6.2, 6.7, 6.7 OL 618, socket ø 6.6, 13.3 mm to step at top of bore, upper body L (−13.3 ø 3.9) 233 (+18.6 ø 10); lower body L (−19.2) 236 (+ inaccessible without dismantling the keywork which crosses it); bell L (− inaccessible) 147 ø 33.3, ext 48.5. Bought from Tony Bingham with *Dragonslayer* fees. On loan to the Bate Collection (*x 245*). [φ 1251/22-24; col sl]. A measured drawing by Tetsu Ito is available.

X   4   Oboe, [crown] / RUDALL / CARTE & Cº LTD / 23 BERNERS STREET / OXFORD STREET / LONDON / 997, post-1911 *(NLI)*. Thumb-plate model to B♭. From hole 2 ø 4.3, 4.3 // 5.1,—(covered by pierced plate), 5.6. OL 571, reed socket ø 7.00, cylindrical to step at top of bore; upper body L (−18 ø 4.25) 221 (+17.2 ø 9.7), lower body L (−17.7) 225 (+16 ø 15.0), bell L (−16.2) 122 ø 37.4, ext 49.6. Bought from William Ring, Worthing, as high pitch and unrepairable but adequate to show this system, the basis of which was patented by Triébert in 1849, and which became that most commonly used in Britain, its principal rival being the later Conservatoire system, devised by Lorée around 1880.

BASSOONS

The curtal (German *Dulzian*) has two bores drilled in one piece of wood, one descending and one ascending, linked at the bottom by a short cross-bore, usually plugged by a piece of cork. It was thus a very compact, space-saving substitute for the bass and contrabass *Pommer* or shawm, with an improved fingering system, which took advantage of its compact, folded shape by adding a second thumb hole (one for each hand) and, in the larger sizes, at least two keys for the thumbs in addition to the extension key for the lower little finger traditional on the bass shawm.

VII   70   Descant curtal, *marked:* [two quatrefoils], which is that of John Cousen, Huddersfield. Acid stained wood, 2 th ø 5.7 slanting down, ø 9 also down, both to the up bore + 7 finger holes ø 5 slanting up, 5 slightly up, 5 down, 5 up, 4.8 horizontal, 4.5 down, 3.8 offset to down bore and straight down—all the others also slant obliquely to the down bore. Short brass crook. OL 412, bore L c. 750 (it depends on the thickness of the base cork, which is not visible) + crook, crook full L 97. Crook ø 4-6.5, socket 7.6, 14.5 to step at top of bore, down bore L (−14.5 ø 5.4) 352; up bore L 402, bell ø 23.5 flaring to c. 35 over c. 10 mm. Width 64.5 from "wing" to bass, Thickness side to side 41.5 at the top of the "wing." This is a reconstruction of the smallest member of the family of the renaissance precursor of the bassoon. The standard size was the bass or *Choristfagott*. On loan to the Bate Collection (*x 356*). Given by the maker when staying with us for the first London Early Instrument Exhibition in 1975. [φ 1246].

The lowest note of the bass curtal was the C on the second ledger line below the bass stave (the eight-foot C). The vital question of the origin of the bassoon, with its added bell which extended the range to the B♭ a tone lower, is still the subject of speculation and controversy. Mersenne, in 1636, refers to an instrument with that range, and it seems probable that the bassoon is earlier than the oboe, rather than later. Much of the evidence for this can be found in Paul White's doctoral thesis. Dr. White also produces convincing evidence for the bassoon's French origin, with Denner as a later maker deriving his model from French and Dutch prototypes such as those by Haka.

The bassoon, like the curtal, differs from all other woodwind in that in addition to its downward bore, from the crook through the wing to the bottom of the butt joint, there is an extension which reaches upwards from the butt to the end of the bell. The downward bore is controlled by six fingerholes, three in the wing and three in the butt, giving a six-finger note of G on the bottom line of the bass stave. A closed key provides the A♭, the equivalent of the oboe's E♭, and an open great key, often with a forked touch like the oboe's C-key, extends the range to F. The upward bore has, on a six-key instrument such as the Goulding here, from the bottom of the butt, a closed key for F♯, a thumbhole for F, closing which produces the low E, and then on the long joint an open key for D, a closed key for E♭, a thumb hole for D, which produces C when closed, and an open key for the bottom B♭. Common additions around 1800 were two harmonic keys at the top of the wing, which acted as speakers and which also steadied notes in the overblown register. The acoustical effect of the upward extension from what would be the lowest note of F if there were no U-bend at the bottom of the butt but an open bell, is that fingering in the upper register tends to be unsystematic and varies from one instrument to another. There are "normal" patterns which may well succeed, but every player learns to experiment when they fail. Don Christlieb, among others, is one who has provided a book of alternative fingerings for awkward notes, high notes, trills, and multiphonics, for his students and colleagues.

The acoustical behaviour, and the tone, is also affected by the very different lengths and diameters of the fingerholes. In order to bring these within the reach of the fingers, they are slanted steeply through the wood. The wing joint is shaped into a wing simply to provide a thicker body so that the inner ends of the fingerholes can be nearer their proper acoustical positions on the bore. Because these holes are long, they must also be narrow in diameter, whereas the holes of the long joint and butt are shorter and wider. The resulting tonal inequality is part of the bassoon's characteristic sound. Applying Boehm's theories to the bassoon, as was done by Marzoli (and earlier on his own theories by Cornelius Ward) led to a wholly key-covered instrument with all the holes much the same diameter and in their acoustically "correct" positions, and a beautifully even tone quality throughout the range. Unfortunately, because the tone was too equal, it no longer sounded like a bassoon! As a result, none of these systems has won general approval, and players and audience alike prefer the traditional inequalities of the bassoon's sound. These inequalities were to some extent smoothed out by Carl Almenräder when he devised the German system bassoon, which was built by Johann Adam Heckel for the firm of Schott, and still further improved by Wilhelm Heckel, the son of Johann Adam, and the grandson Wilhelm Hermann, the leading manufacturers of that system. The German system, which is that most widely used internationally today, is somewhat safer and more reliable than the French system, but the latter remains much closer to the earlier instrument in both sound and behaviour. It was developed principally by Jean Nicholas Savary, an unrivalled sequence of whose instruments may be seen in the Bate Collection. The French system was used in Britain into the 1930s, and a few players adhered to it even into the 1960s, but today, even in France, it is all-but extinct, though one always hears of interest in its revival for the sake of its much livelier and more interesting tone colour.

II   62   Bassoon, *marked:* [lyre] / GOULDING / PALL MALL / LON-

DON, c. 1799 *(NLI)*. Maple with brass mounts and 6 keys for BB♭, D, E♭, F, F♯ and A♭. Wing fingerholes: 4.3, 5, 4.7 // butt 4.5, 5.5, 4.7, th 7.9 // long joint th 8.5. The butt is closed by a simple cork. Crook stamped IH 4 (John Hale), no pin hole. OL 1254, crook tip internal ø 4.5, end 10.5, socket ø 15.5, conical to top of bore; wing L (−83 ø 10.5) 478 (+46.2 ø 15.7), butt L (−46.5) 412 + 412 (−46); long joint L (+45.7 ø 25.2) 497 (+41.5 ø 29.9 × 31.2), bell L (−42.7) 323 ø 41.8; no choke but cylindrical most of the way. Sling ring missing. Illustrated in my *Romantic & Modern* pl. X; *PTY* no 5. Bought at a Puttick & Simpson auction without having observed that a previous owner had removed the wing from the butt while leaving the tenon in its socket. An excellent repair was carried out by James Howarth. [φ 1234/Q/13-14; b/w slides front and back; col sl; colour 120].

George Goulding was a dealer and while he may have made pianos and organs *(NLI)* it is doubtful whether he ever made any woodwind instruments. James Wood was one of his woodwind makers, as was John Hale, three of whose bassoons are known, but whose best known work was as a key and crook maker to the trade. Many instruments marked by other makers have keys and other parts marked IH—it is of course possible that this is an indication that Hale made the whole instrument for whoever stamped his name on it, and that may therefore be true in this case.

II   60   Bassoon, *marked:* [maltese cross] / EXCELSIOR / SONOROUS / CLASS / HAWKES & SON / DENMAN STREET / PICCADILLY CIRCUS / LONDON / 4145 [cross]; post-1895 *(NLI)*. Rosewood, white bronze keys and mounts. Bell unmarked and paler wood. Shield-shape plaque removed from the top of the wing. 16 keys + crook key (no separate touch). Normal French system (see the drawing here, which as well as showing the keys shows by means of arrows the direction that the holes take through the wood). The keys and holes in succession from the top of the wing are: crook key, closed by opening any of the next three; three trill + harmonic keys, the lowest of them the "Creation key" for a tricky rapid alternation in that work; f fingerhole (ø 5), a fourth vent and trill key, e hole (5.7), e♭ key, d hole (5.7), c♯ key. Then on the butt the c hole (6.7), the B hole (7.2) and the A hole (6.2), followed by the B♭ key, which opens into the upward bore—all the keys so far are closed keys—and the open F key and closed A♭ key, which also go to the upward bore and which are fitted with rollers to make it easier to move from one to the other. On the thumb side we have, from the bottom of the butt, the closed F♯ key and the F hole (8.5). On the long joint, there is the open D key, the closed E♭, the open C key, which closes also the D key, the closed C♯, the open BB♭, which closes also the C and D keys, and the closed BB♮. The C key is a round plate and the touches of the other five keys all cluster round or beneath it, for they are all operated by the left thumb. H pattern piercing on the D-key guard. It was very common for bassoon makers to pierce this key-guard with a pattern formed by their initials, and this is sometimes the only way to identify the maker of an otherwise unmarked instrument. The butt is closed by a cork plug under a hinged flap, with a brass plate above and below the cork, the inner plate curved to fit the bore. The cork is removed with a pull ring. OL 1291, crook tip ø 4.5, end 8.8, metal-lined socket ø 12.8, cylindrical to step at top of bore; wing L (-25.25 ø 9.2) 455 (+38.3 ø 15.2), butt L (−39.25) 394 + 391 (−39.25), long joint L (+39.4 ø 25.4) 519 (+39.4 ø 32.8, bell L (−38.8) 338 ø 52.9 (the discrepancy between the length of the bell socket and the long joint upper tenon suggests that it may not be wholly a coincidence that the wood of the bell is a different colour from the rest of the instrument). Bought Puttick & Simpson auction 27/7/61. Illustrated in my *Romantic & Modern* pl.XI. [φ 1234/Q/15-16; b/w sl; colour 120/2].

VII 224 Bassoon, GBR. ALEXANDER / MAINZ, wing overstamped in cursive letters: Alexander / in / Mainz; c. 1870. Rosewood and white bronze, ivory bell ring (cracked), music holder receiver (screw missing) on crook socket. Cork-lapped silver crook (not original) with sticking-plaster covering the pin hole (there is no crook key). The wing socket of the butt is metal lined; the long joint socket is not. Almenräder system pre-1880. On the wing joint, from the top on the finger-side, there are three fingerholes for f, e, and d, the f sloping sharply upwards and the d sloping downwards, ø 4.7, 5.5, and 4.9 and, on the thumb-side, three closed keys, two towards the top for c′ and a, which also act as harmonic keys, and the third at the bottom of the joint for c♯; their touches of course cluster together opposite those of the thumb keys on the long joint. On the butt joint, on the finger side, there are two fingerholes for c and B, ø 5.4 and 6.5, followed by, in the order of their touches, a lever which controls a pin passing through the wood to open a key on the thumb side for B♭, a touch which closes a double-headed key for G, the upper keyhead covering a hole to the upward bore and the lower to the downward. The next touch closes a hole for F in the upward bore, and is itself closed by opening the F♯ key, also to the upward bore, whose touch overlaps it. The lowest touch opens a key to the bottom of the upward bore for A♭. On the thumb side, from the bottom, the lowest touch opens a key to the downward bore for G♯ (in normal practice by no means the same note as A♭), and the next opens a key for F♯, to the upward bore. A short lever closes a key to the upward bore for E, and the highest touch opens the B♭ key which is also opened by the pin coming through from the fingerside, which was noted above.

The butt is sufficiently complex, with its two bores in the one piece of wood, that it may be useful to recapitulate, this time taking the holes, rather than the touches, in order from the top of the downward bore, i.e., continuing from the c♯ key at the bottom of the wing. First are the two fingerholes for c and B, followed by one head of the double-headed open key for G. Then, from the bottom of the upward bore, the closed key for A♭, the open key for F, the other head of the open G key, the two closed F♯ keys, that for the thumb slightly lower than that for the little finger, the closed B♭ key which is opened from either side, and finally the open key for E, which covers what was the thumb hole on the earlier systems with fewer keys. On the long joint there is, from the bottom, an open thumb key for D, a closed key for the little finger for E♭, an open thumb key for C which also, of course, closes the D key. Next a closed key for C♯, whose touch for the little finger lies beside that for E♭. The touch for the BB♮ key overlaps the C key so that when the BB♮ key is closed it also closes both the C key and the D key. Finally, beside the touch for the BB♮ key is that for BB♭ so that both can be closed by the thumb and the instrument's lowest note can speak out of the bell.

It may be worth reiterating, even at the risk of confusion, that whereas fingerholes are named for the notes which speak out of them (i.e., when they are opened), keys are named for the notes which result when they are moved from their position of rest. As a result, a closed key is named, like a fingerhole, for the note which speaks out of it when it is opened (by moving it from its position of rest). An open key, however, is different. When one closes, on the long joint, the D key, moving it from its position of rest, the note D can speak out of the C hole; thus on earlier systems when the hole in the centre of the long joint was simply a thumbhole, that was the D hole because D spoke out of it. Once, with the addition of keywork, a key was put over that hole, that key became the C key because by closing it the low C was sounded.

The butt is closed by a brass U-bend which slides off to open it. It is covered by a pull-off cap which must be slightly too tight a fit, for the base of the U-bend is slightly flattened. OL 1260, crook ø 3.8-8.5, socket 11.3, wing L (−23.3 ø 8.5) 480 (+36 ø 16.5), butt L (−38) 386 + 386 (−42), long joint L (+41.5 ø 24.5) 537 (+39 ø 33, cracked), bell L (−40) 331 ø 37.1 before final flare over 10 mm to

42.5, 66 ext. On loan to the Bate Collection (*x 337*). Bought from Stuart Brown. [φ 1248].

For further details of the development and history of the oboe and bassoon, see my *World of Baroque & Classical Musical Instruments* and *World of Romantic & Modern Musical Instruments,* and my Bate Collection *Double Reed* Guide. Also, and better, Anthony Baines *Woodwind Instruments and their History,* Faber, 1957 *et seq.* and Philip Bate *The Oboe,* Benn, 1956 *et seq.* We still need a good book on the history of the bassoon.

REEDS

With the global expansion of reed-playing, especially of clarinets and saxophones, the ever-increasing atmospheric pollution, and the greed of reed-manufacturers in not allowing adequate time for reeds to season, the quality of reed cane deteriorates year by year. Any experienced professional player will agree that reed is not what it was, whether he is a double-reed player (most of whom make their own reeds from raw cane) or a single-reed player (most of whom buy reeds by the box-full and throw away 90 percent of them as unusable—a practise almost incomprehensible to oboists and bassoonists). Thus the successful invention of a reed of artificial material is becoming more and more urgent. So far nothing has appeared that a serious professional would use, but that does not mean that the task is impossible; only that the right material has not yet been found. It seems probable that the materials so far tried have been too uniform; a natural reed consists of a sloping section through the bark and each layer below it, each of which responds in a different way, as can be seen in Paul White's drawings. Only when artificial materials can reproduce the response of each individual layer of the natural material, and when each is proportioned as it would be by a master reed-maker, can one expect it to succeed. Let us hope that one day this will be achieved.

X   154   Reeds for orchestral instruments, not yet fully itemised, including: plastic reeds for oboe and bassoon (the latter on loan to the Bate Collection); 15 german bassoon, 1 french bassoon, 1 contra-bassoon; 2 cor anglais, 9 oboe, 4 early-style oboe, Eric Halfpenny's copper staple for the Milhouse oboe, 5 musette (thread bound, not cork lapped); 2 staples, 2 gouged canes, 1 gouged and shaped cane, 3 gouged, shaped, and folded canes, 1 plaque, 1 mandrel, all for oboe. Also a single-reed mouthpiece for bassoon with 9 reeds, on loan to the Bate Collection.

The single-reed mouthpiece is much stronger, especially when playing on the march, and more useful for many purposes, and examples are known from the early nineteenth century, perhaps before, and certainly thereafter. How generally they were then used is not known; it is possible that they were church-band mouthpieces, for it would certainly be possible for amateur bassoonists to cobble up a single reed for such a mouthpiece more easily than making a conventional double reed from materials locally available. Similar mouthpieces for oboe and cor anglais are much rarer and may only be fairly modern devices.

X   156   Reeds for non-orchestral instruments, not yet fully itemised, including bagpipes: set for *gaita gallega*, 3 Scots drone (single) reeds, 2 Scots plastic practice-chanter reeds, 1 plastic chanter reed.

Shawms: 3 *guan*, 1 *hichiriki*, 2 *mey*, 1 *balaban*, 1 *hnè* from John Okell, 1 *pī nai* from Ferre de Hen, 4 Indian in a holder, 2 in the holder for V 48, and 5 other Indian one of them on a long staple, 13 Chinese of varying sizes, 7 from Gwen Plumley for the Egyptian *mizmar*, 2 Turkish, 5 Moroccan, including materials not made up and a staple, 2 from the Madauchi for the *algaita*, 1 Batak, 3 for the less good *dolçaina*, 3 from Vicent Torrent for the better one, 3 from Jon Swayne for the *ciaramella*, 1 from Xavier Auriols for the *gralla*, 2 from the Early Music Shop for the "mediæval" shawm, 3 from the Bath Early Music Shop for the *bombarde*. There are almost certainly more which have escaped notice at this stage, and there are others standing in instruments.

Part II
Single Reeds

IDIOGLOT PERCUSSION-REED "WHISTLES"–412.12

Whereas the concussion reed, such as the oboe and bassoon reed and others described under Double Reeds, has two like elements which beat together and both of which vibrate equally, the percussion reed is called a single reed because it has a single vibrating element which beats on a non-vibrating body, for example a brass blade beating on the metal shallot of an organ reed-pipe or a slip of bamboo beating against the wooden or plastic mouthpiece of the clarinet or saxophone.

When the reed is cut from, or moulded integrally with, the body of the mouthpiece, the term idioglot or idioglottal (*idio*-self; *glot*-tongue) is used; when a separate reed is tied on, it is heteroglot (*hetero*-other). A problem arises with the instruments made of reed or cane, such as the *zummāra*, with an idioglottal reed (see III 38c) which is sometimes integral with the instrument (e.g., VIII 150) but sometimes cut idioglottally in a separate mouthpiece; we need a distinct term for the mouthpiece so that it becomes either "truly idioglot" or else "idioglot-hetero-?". *Zeugos* seems the nearest name (see Heinz Becker) that the Greeks had for the mouthpiece of the *aulos*, as distinct from the reed, the vibrating element, or the *holmos*, the part of the instrument into which the *zeugos* was inserted. The vast majority of instruments of this type are idioglot-heterozeug, with a small bamboo tube, the "zeug," with a tongue cut in it idioglottally, inserted into the top of a tube with fingerholes. This is an obviously sensible method of construction because reeds wear out in time, and when that of VIII 150 does so, the instrument will become useless and a whole new instrument will have to be made, with fingerholes bored, tuned, and so on. When the reed of a heterozeug instrument wears out, a new zeug can be made, with a new reed cut in it, and inserted into the top of the instrument; indeed some of those under 422.22 have spare zeugs attached for precisely this reason, ready for instant use.

It is arguable that we have here a developmental sequence, for it would seem probable that the truly idioglottal instruments are the earlier in development, the result of the invention or accidental discovery of such a reed, allied with the invention of fingerholes, and that after the experience and annoyance, over a period of unknown length, perhaps of millennia, of throwing away perfectly good instruments just because a reed has broken, it occurred to someone to cut off the proximal end with its broken reed and insert a new mouthpiece separately made (heterozeug) of a short piece of cane.

Whether the idioglottal mouthpiece be idiozeug or heterozeug, obviously the proximal end must be closed, normally by a node of the reed or cane from which it is made, but sometimes by an inserted plug of pith, wax, or other material. If the end were open, the air would go straight down the tube without forcing the reed to vibrate. Only by compelling the air to pass between the reed and the zeug, so lifting the reed from the zeug, the tongue from the body from which it is partly cut, can the reed be made to vibrate and thus to sound.

Reeds can be either downcut or upcut. Upcut, with the hinge towards the closed upper end (fig. 1, front view and profile), is the more common and is obviously preferable, for if the cut starts to spread with vibration, as it is liable to do, then it cannot easily spread far (which would flatten the pitch as the tongue lengthens), nor, because it is held at the node, is it so likely to break off. The downcut reed (fig. 2), however, does have the advantage that the player can bridle the reed with the lips and so control its pitch, as is done with thread on the Highland bagpipe drone reed and others, and control also, to some extent, its freedom of vibration and thus its tone quality. However, vibration does encourage the cut of the reed to extend and, with the downcut reed, eventually simply to split off the end of the zeug. With the upcut reed, the player must, of course, place the whole mouthpiece in the mouth, with the lips beyond the free end of the reed, since touching it with the lips would prevent it from vibrating.

Such reeds can be tuned in a number of ways. Obviously, the longer the reed or the greater its mass (in practise its width and/or its thickness, especially its thickness at the free end), the more sluggish its vibration and thus the lower the pitch. Thinning the reed at or near its hinge makes it vibrate more easily, thus making it easier to blow, though at the same time weakening it at precisely the point where it is most liable to break. Blobs of tuning wax at or near the free end are often seen, and these of course lower the pitch by adding to the mass, just as does leaving the reed thicker at that point. As Laurence Picken points out (*LERP*, p. 509), this also darkens the tone by reducing the higher frequencies. A bridle can be tied round the reed to fix its length, on simpler examples, or held against it by a spring wire, on organ pipes, and moved along it to alter the vibrating length and thus the pitch. Reeds which are stiff or heavy, and therefore reluctant to sound, can be encouraged by slipping a hair from the player's beard or moustache (such hairs are usually thicker than scalp-hairs and thus more effective) between the reed and the body, close to the hinge, holding them very slightly apart and so making the reed more willing to begin to vibrate.

See 422.211 below for further information about the instruments with which such reeds are used.

III 38c Giant version of a *zummāra* idioglot/heterozeug mouthpiece made of bamboo for demonstration. The proximal end is closed by a natural node of the cane, and a tongue, the reed, painted red to distinguish it, has been cut away from the body, the zeug, cutting towards the proximal end ("upcut"). This reed is too large to blow in the conventional manner, with the whole body down to and including the free end of the reed enclosed within the mouth cavity, but when blown in reverse, from the open end of the tube, the reed vibrates and shows how the mouthpiece functions. OL 277; reed L c. 115; ø ext 34.6; int 25.5. [φ 1234/J/34; b/w slide].

XI 254 A second, somewhat smaller example, which was made to put on display in the Bate Collection, has now (September 1997) been given to the Bate.

III 134g A number of reedpipes made for demonstration, bamboo with an integral idioglot reed, some with and some without fingerholes. Only one of these could be found (March 1997); others were presumably given away at demonstrations to show how simple such reeds are and how easily they are made, or are lurking elsewhere. The distal end of this one has been shaved down as though to fit into an instrument; there is no fingerhole. OL 58.9; reed L c. 16; bore ø 5.

IX 106 Plastic cock with windmill; *marked:* Made in W. Germany. Idioglot downcut single reed moulded integrally in a yellow plastic mouthpiece in the tail of a green plastic silhouette of a cock. As the player blows, the red plastic wheel with 12 spokes, which represents the tail feathers, acts as a windmill and spins round. The pitch of the reed, and the speed of the wheel, depend on the air pressure. A child's toy demonstrating acoustical principles. OL (mouthpiece to cock's beak) 138; reed L c. 19. Given by my wife, eighth day Chanukah (Christmas eve) 1984; she had bought it for one of the grandchildren, but it was clearly a useful addition to the collection, showing both aurally and visually how airspeed and pitch are linked.

XII	38	Another, *marked:* C E / Made in Germany / Bruder. Red plastic cock, blue windmill with 12 spokes, cream mouthpiece with idioglot reed. OL 137; reed L c. 19. Bought more recently from Hawkin, Harleston (a major importer of cheap toys, many of them musical), with a second given to M-Antònia Juan.
X	126	Plastic *shofar*. Off-white plastic, moulded in two halves, glued together (not moulded together); heterozeug mouthpiece and idioglot reed transparent brownish plastic. One side (player's right) moulded MADE IN ISRAEL /#/ HAPPY NEW YEAR; the other [l'shanah tovah = to a good year]. The bell is the typical Euro-Ashkenazi hooked shape; the underside with square "step" indentations which seem to be characteristic of *shofarot* of First Aliyah date (e.g., X 14). Made so that children as young as possible can, at least in play, share in performing the commandment to blow the *shofar*. Further details of the *shofar* and its use will be found in the relevant fascicle of this catalogue, dealing with Horns. OL 229; L round outside of curve c. 310; bell ø 39.5 × 17; pitch indeterminate. Bought in an educational shop in a cellar in Mea Shearim, Jerusalem.
IX	182	Plastic reed-horn, Finland. Bilious green and white plastic imitating a traditional coiled bark instrument which is blown either as a whithorn (cf VI 80 in 412.11) or as a trumpet. With heterozeug idioglot plastic single reed. OL 254; L round outside of curve c. 280; reed L 14; pitch f♯''-30 cents. Bought in a music shop in Helsinki during the ICTM Conference.
XII	122d	Toy trumpet, blue plastic zeug containing an idioglot plastic single reed marked TENA, silver paper conical body with multi-coloured paper streamers. OL 280 + streamers;

plastic head L 62.5. Given by my grandaughter, Kate Rose-man, who was kind enough to accumulate several such toy instruments on my behalf during a family party.

XII   130   Yellow plastic zeug with red coiled paper, lined on the inner side of the coil with blue paper with silver stars. A toy trumpet that straightens out as one blows and then coils up again. Idioglot plastic reed, working only on blow. OL 312; mouthpiece L 40. Source unknown.

XII   132a/b   Blue plastic zeug with an idioglot reed which works only on suck. Traces of a red compound round the base of the zeug. Presumably from a balloon which would squeak as it de-flated. (b) another identical but green, with fragments of green balloon adhering. No known source. OL 35 for each.

HETEROGLOT SINGLE-REED "WHISTLES"

V   214a/b   Two organ reeds, the one with the longer stub of pipe re-maining (a) stamped F on the side of the shallot; the other (b) stamped G♯. The block, reed, shallot, tuning bridle, and a very short length of the pipe only. The reed of (a) is held in place by a wooden wedge between it and the socket. The socket is a lead alloy; the shallot and reed are brass; the bri-dle is ferrous. The wooden wedge is missing from (b) and the long, thin, narrowly-tapering reed is held in place only by the bridle, so more measurements were possible. The boot is also missing from each. Pipe stub L (a) 48.4, (b) 17.7; shallot L (a) 50.6, (b) 48; max ø of shallot both 10.3. Reed of (b) L 57; W 1.3 to 5.8; Th 0.3. Slot in the shallot of (b) L 19.5; W 1.0 to 4.1. Rescued from an "antique" dealer in Peckham, who had ripped off the pipes to convert them into pseudo coach horns. [φ (a) 6260/8/8-9].

Both show well how the organ reed works, and the function of the tuning bridle, and the fact that a very small movement of the bridle makes a very considerable difference to the pitch obtained. It is regrettable that I got two neighbouring pipes; two which had been further apart in pitch would have been more interesting.

With organ reedpipes, it is the reed which determines the pitch; the pipe is a coupled resonator whose shape etc determines the tone, and thus the name of the rank or stop to which it belongs, but not the pitch. It is on this, somewhat shaky basis that Hornbostel & Sachs placed the organ reed pipes in 41 rather than in 42 (Wind Instruments Proper).

I   142a   Fog horn, W. NUNN & CO / MANUFACTURERS / LONDON, brass now heavily oxidised, with folded longitudinal seam. Originally screwed into something at a flange about one third of the length from the reed end, presumably a mechanical sounding apparatus because the use of mouth-blown foghorns was banned on British ships for safety reasons by the Board of Trade in 1880, and this horn may have been a result of this ban. The boot or socket must have been at least 160 mm long. The reed is inaccessible but can be seen to be heavy brass on a hemi-cylinder shallot. OL 373; proximal end ø c. 21; bell 50.5 int, 56.7 ext. Bought from Paxman. [φ 1234/P/14].

I   142b   Fog horn originally with a tie-on label (now disintegrated) which read: "Short Brass Horn, Bt. Frangiolini Nov 29th 1933." An original name plate has been removed. Mouth-blown. Folded seam. The reed is inaccessible, but it is assumed to be of the same sort as the previous. The prohibition of mouthblown foghorns referred to in the previous entry was widely ignored in small boats and on private yachts; as a result, many were run down and sunk in bad weather while a sailor tried, with frozen fingers and lips, to get a sound from a mouth-blown foghorn. OL 495; prox end ø c. 11; bell 64.3 × 55.3. Also bought from Paxman. [φ 1234/P/13].

I   142c   Warning horn, Acme, Birmingham. Modern version of a and b. Chromium plated brass. Marked THE ACME / MADE IN / ENGLAND /#/ THOMAS FOULKES / LEYTONSTONE. Horn shaped with curved body in a flattened cone; two loops on the concave side for a suspension cord. Brass reed on a brass shallot. Screw-on reed cap with protective gauze over the proximal end. See below (III 112i) for a note on Acme. OL 296; prox end ø 18.2; bell 68.6 × 36.4; reed L 53; W 13.6;

Th 0.3. Bought from Foulkes (a yacht chandler in the Lea Valley). [φ 1234/B/18].

III   112g   Motor horn with black rubber bulb, c. 1920. The bugle shape, conical horn of black-painted brass has a wire gauze over the wide end to keep pebbles and other debris out of it. A long rubber tube links the bulb to the horn; the bulb was fitted on the body of the car within the driver's reach (the screw for the clamp at this end is missing), and the horn was fixed as near the front as possible. The bulb is now perished and even when it was new, more than thirty years after it was made, the horn was more reliable when mouth-blown; when used for musical purposes one may need to sound it exactly on the beat, and the bulb was always a bit too sluggish for that—musically precise timing is not so essential when used on a motor car. The brass reed is on a brass shallot with a tube screwed over it, adjustable for length, both to protect it and to receive the end of the rubber tube. OL 1070 (originally more when the bellows was not crumpled); tube L c. 620; reed L 56.5; horn OL 245 (excluding the reed). Bought new from a garage in Northampton for use in a pantomime (if not for Cinderella's coach, certainly for Baron Hardup's and other vehicles); the original cardboard box, now lost, said "as fitted for Rolls Royce." On loan to the Bate Collection (*x 4082*). [φ 1234/E/39; b/w slide].

Motor horns are a necessary part of any percussion player's stock of instruments, for they are needed not only for pantomimes but also for more serious works such as Gershwin's *An American in Paris*; just as we all bring gongs for a work by Messiaen or other gong-ho composers, and then choose the best or the most suitable from among them, so we all bring motor horns for the Gershwin and pick the best-matched pair.

The reeds of such horns, like those of the fog horns, are no different from those of the toy trumpets and other noise-makers, and little different from those of organ pipes, save that they are not normally tunable. They differ only in material and method of manufacture from those of the more "musical" instruments among the single reeds, such as clarinets and saxophones.

It is a solidly based convention that all noise-makers are included among the musical instruments, classified under the same criteria. This

convention arose because they belong together scientifically and acoustically, but it applies also in musical practice when composers include motor
horns in their scores, and sirens (e.g., Edgar Varèse in *Ionisation*), typewrit-
ers and aeroplane engines (Georges Antheil in several works), sandpaper
blocks (Paul Hindemith in *Klein Kammermusik Nr 1*), iron chains (Arnold
Schönberg in *Gurrelieder* and Henry Litolff in his *Robespierre* Overture),
spurs (Johann Strauss in *Die Fledermaus*), ratchets (Beethoven in *Wellingtons
Sieg oder die Schlacht bei Vittoria*, the *Battle Symphony*), and there are many
other such objects listed in the repertoire before one even begins to con-
sider the more modern composers and the more ephemeral requirements
of the film and television studios.

III	112k	Motor horn with bulb, straight model, the bulb missing. Brass reed on a brass shallot. Cylindrical reed holder plated, conical horn black-painted brass with gauze over the wide end to protect it. OL 223; reed holder ø 18.5; horn ø 41.5 to 74.5. [φ 1234/E/8; b/w slide].
IX	136	Motor horn, bulb missing. The horn plated, the screw-off reed holder green painted. Large brass reed on a brass shal-lot at the end of a tube coiled helically round its own bell; the bell marked 80/3. Helix L 73; OW 170; bell ø 82; reed L 42.5, W 12.5. Bought at a Phillips auction, Oxford as part of a box of drummer's effects.
XII	162	Single-reed horn, unmarked. Straight brass bell with neatly soldered longitudinal seam, the end rolled over. A loop spotsoldered on holding a split ring for suspension. Chromium plated or white bronze mouthpiece unscrews. Brass reed on black plastic shallot (i.e., not as old as it looks). OL 112, bell L 77, end ø 24 (internal); reed L 17, W 8.5. Bought Abilads, Thursday open market, Oxford.
III	114b	Squeaker, Acme, Birmingham. Conical black plastic tube in two parts, mouthpipe and bell, the bell containing a brass single reed on a hemi-cylindrical brass shallot like that of a motor horn. OL 82.5; mouthpipe L 52.5, ø 11 to 17.5; bell L 29.7 + tenon 8.4 + reed L 24.5, W 7.2, Th 0.2; bell ø 21.6. [φ 1234/F/25].
III	114c	Squeaker, Acme, Birmingham. Chromium-plated metal tube with flattened end for a mouthpiece, containing a

brass single reed on a hemi-cylindrical brass shallot, held in place with a screw through the side; not dismantled for measuring. OL 92; ø 18; mouthpiece 23.5 × 6. [φ 1234/F/24].

IX 160 Rooster Crow, Besson & Co, London. Brass cylindrical tube with a brass single reed on a hemi-cylindrical brass shallot. *Marked:* ROOSTER CROW / Form a trumpet with the hands / at the end of the tube and imitate / in blowing the rhythm of the / crow, blowing louder and longer / for the last note / BESSON & CO Ltd, London. Besson's London branch became a limited company in 1896 and survived until taken over by Boosey & Hawkes in 1948 (*NLI*). OL 101.5; ø 12.7. Bought at Phillips auction, Oxford as part of a box of drummer's effects.

III 112j Bicycle horn, rubberized canvas bulb with a metal cap faintly stamped PATENT No. 669313 / ACUMEN; the bulb containing a powerful spring and the reed, the bell missing. The reed is inaccessible, but it is probably a single reed of the same type as the rest. OL 115, cap ø 64.5. [φ 1234/E/8].

IX 154a Toy trumpet. A brass cone with a copper single reed, fixed much as on IX 156 (*infra*), marked KITCHEN / & Cº / LEEDS on the bell; Kitchen was the major musical instrument shop in Leeds from the 1890s onward, and was presumably the seller rather than the maker. A short cylindrical mouthpipe is soldered over the end of a conical metal bell whose soldered longitudinal seam is almost invisible; a much better quality instrument than the following three. OL 147; mouthpipe L 40, ø 11.7; bell L 106, ø 31 int, 35.5 ext; pitch c♯′.

The provision of instruments *en pacotille*, unmarked so that wholesalers or retailers can mark them for their own credit, is widespread and goes back certainly to the eighteenth century and quite possibly earlier. Many, possibly all, unmarked instruments result from this practice, a maker supplying a dealer who did not bother to stamp his own mark on the instrument. This is the probable origin of many of the instruments which were marked by general dealers such as Goulding, Longman & Broderip,

Clementi, and others. The tradition continues into our own day, with major retailers importing cheap instruments in bulk from China and other low-cost areas and marking them with their own names or with names registered for that purpose. A number of examples of this practice will be found in this catalogue.

IX   154b   Toy trumpet. Brassed tinplate cone, rolled over, the seam neither soldered nor folded, with a brass single reed on a metal shallot in the end, unmarked. OL 134; mouthpipe ø 6.5, bell 24.5; pitch eʰ'.

IX   154c   Toy trumpet. Similar to (b) but smaller, with most of the brass worn off. OL 109; mouthpipe ø 6, bell 21.5; pitch f♯'.

IX   154d   Toy trumpet. Similar again but smaller still. OL 85; mouthpipe ø 5.5, bell 10.5; pitch aʰ'.

IX   124a-c   3 wooden toy trumpets. Turned cone of white wood, each with a brass single reed on a brass shallot, (a) painted with 2 bands of red paint and 1 of blue and 2 narrow blue rings above the slightly flared bell; (b) smaller with 2 bands of red paint and 4 blue rings; (c) smallest with 2 bands of blue, one of red, and 2 red rings. OL (a) 125, (b) 111, (c) 76; prox end ø (a) 11.5, (b) 7.5, (c) 13; bell ø (a) 20.5 int 27.7 ext, (b) 16.5 and 21.5, (c) 10 & 12; pitch (a) c‴, (b) e‴, (c) e‴.

The toy trumpet is normally simply that; a child's toy which produces a single pitch. They were widely used in the latter part of the nineteenth century and can be seen in many illustrations in children's books of that period. Some are more overtly trumpet-shape, as are many plastic toys today, but others are short metal or wooden tubes of this sort. Most composers of a *Toy Symphony* have included one or more in the score, and there are instruments manufactured, and available for hire with the band parts, which will produce the pitches demanded by "Haydn" and others. The examples here, however, are more likely to be simply toys, perhaps with the exception of the instrument from Kitchen, and they all probably date from the latter part of the nineteenth or early twentieth centuries. They were all bought at a Phillips, Oxford, auction in a box of drummer's effects.

VI   104   Child's toy in the form of a snake of 12 jointed plastic segments (each green above and white below, linked with steel pins), with a small metal single-reed, well down and wholly inaccessible in the longer tail joint. The head segment has a long, red, forked tongue and 2 eyes, the pupils of which are lead shot which roll around under transparent plastic domes. The segments are so jointed that the snake forms a semi-circle in one plane and can take any shape in the other. OL round curve c. 335; tail joint L 69; other segments L 24. Bought at the Todaiji Temple, Nara, Japan. Given by Laurence Picken; his CUMAE 77.357. Laurence Picken and I used to buy cheap instruments in duplicate as gifts for each other; I benefited greatly from his round-the-world tour. His own collection went to the Cambridge University Museum of Archæology and Ethnography in 1977. [φ 14/6/5].

X   198   Doll cry, England. Ceramic weight moulded integrally MADE IN ENGLAND / S25/5 with a single reed in a green plastic pot with a pink top. The bellows, which were probably a condom, have now perished. As the doll is turned over, the weight pushes the bellows closed so that the reed sounds in an approximation to ma-ma, a baby's cry. The very flexible small copper reed is on the underside of the weight (where it cannot be seen unless the pot is opened) and is bridled with thread. A small air hole goes through the ceramic weight to the upper side, which would be all that was normally visible through the holes in the pink top. This is so much the appearance of the cow and lamb baa XI 298 that it is assumed (in preference to destroying them by taking them apart) that they work in the same way. The base of the pot is moulded MADE IN ENGLAND / RB S/30 / PAT APP. OL 55; ø 40.5; reed L 14, free L c. 7, W c. 4.

On most of these toys, the reed is sufficiently flexible that variation of air pressure or speed produces variation of pitch (as demonstrated by X 198 above), thus adding a variety of pitch, appealing to the children for whose entertainment most are designed.

XI   298a-c   Three children's animal noises. Similar to a doll-cry; each consists of a cylindrical plastic box containing a weight, a bellows perhaps, as often, made of a condom, and a reed, or in one case here a widgeon whistle (a). As the box is inverted, the weight pulls the bellows open; as it is inverted again, the weight drives the air through the reed. Each is covered in a pictorial label; each has a pierced plastic grill top; and each is marked Made in Taiwan on the base. Without opening them, the type of reed cannot be determined for certain, but (b) and (c) are so similar to X 198 that it is a reasonable assumption that they are the same.

a) pictures of birds; marked Chen Ming. Produces bird-like whistles from, judging by the sound, a widgeon or labial whistle similar to those made of fruit kernels, and therefore not belonging in this catalogue but included here as part of the set.

b) pictures of cows and marked COW / CM112-1. Moos. The air hole is central.

c) pictures of lambs. Baas. The air hole is at the side, like that of X 198.

All three were bought at the London Piano Museum, Brentford. All three OH 51.5; ø 52.5.

III   112i   Hooter, Acme, Birmingham. Chromium-plated metal tube containing a single reed. 2 cylindrical telescopic tubes, the outer simply a holder, the inner with a long black plastic shallot with a long, wide, thin, and very flexible, brass reed. OL 110 to 130; outer L 85.5, ø 22.4; inner L 50 + shallot L 50, ø 20.4; reed L 45, W 12.3 at widest, Th 0.3. [φ 1234/F/17].

Acme make a wide variety of noise makers, some for fun, some for work, including the famous Acme Thunderer referee's pea-whistle. See also the fog- or warning-horn (I 142c) and the squeakers (III 114) above. Some of their products imitate bird and animal cries for hunters, and are game lures. Others of their noise makers, like this one, seem made simply to make a noise. Various of these have been bought either from interest, or earlier in my career as percussion kit, for which a wide variety of noises and effects is always essential equipment.

V   138b   Goose Call, Black Duck, Whiting, Indiana. Wooden un-marked two-part holder. Black plastic shallot with a long, thin, black reed of either metal or plastic wedged in position by a smaller piece of plastic. The length of the reed is adjustable, and it may be double-ended so that it can be turned round if one end is damaged. OL 144; mouthpipe L 96.5, ø 16.2; other part L 56.5 + shallot 49; exposed L of reed 29. Bought in Harry's Sport Shop, Grinnell, Iowa, 1970. [φ 6260/8/5].

V   138c   MALLARDTONE / [bird in flight] / CROW / CALL. 2901 16th St, Moline, Illinois. Plastic reed beating two ways between two pieces of wood, so that it forms a single reed with a shallot on each side, in a wooden holder. OL 122; mouthpiece L 44.5. Bought as (b). [φ 6260/8/2-3].

V   138d   MALLARDTONE / [animal face] / COON / CALL. A wooden holder with an insert of two pieces of white wood, each with a longitudinal groove, with 3 plastic blades sandwiched between them; the two outer blades are longer than the middle one which seems to act as a spacer between them so that each of the longer ones can act as a single reed to its piece of wood. It is difficult to determine which piece of plastic is doing what to which, but I think that each is a single reed. OL 118; insert L 64; reed L 57.5, W 12.8. Provenance as (b). [φ 6260/8/4].

All three of these are accompanied by detailed instruction sheets (the first headed Black Duck Game Calls / "Master of Sound" / 1737 Davis Avenue / Whiting, Ind. 46394 / phone 219–659-2997) describing the technique required to produce a realistic imitation; also by a catalogue of all the calls available and of 45 rpm records which illustrate the noises to aim at, something that requires considerable skill, often involving the precise shaping of variable capacity resonance air bodies with the hand or hands. The calls themselves are remarkably similar to, although much smaller than, the wooden reed instruments of the Canadian North-West Coast Indians. So much so that one wonders whether these North-West Coast reed instruments may also have been animal and bird imitators, connected with the totemistic rituals of that area, rather than strictly musical instruments or random noise-makers. See F. W. Galpin "Whistles and Reeds" for descriptions of these instruments, and the general anthropological literature on that area for the totemistic aspects of the culture. The North-West Coast instruments have reeds with large wooden blades, shaved down from softwoods such as pine, cedar, and spruce, whereas the reeds of the instruments here are much smaller and of plastic, but the principles are very similar.

IX 156 Wooden hooter. Well made heavy beech cylinder, with a separate reedcap. A piece of thin copper sheet is fixed in a slit over the end of the body tube, which is cut off obliquely, and bent to cover the end of the tube. The copper was cut quite roughly with snips and is secured with a small screw to make a form of single reed. OL 237; mouthpipe L 104; body L 133 + tenon which forms the shallot, L 38.3 to 54.7; reed L 17, W 12.5, th 0.3; tenon bore ø 9; body bore 14. Bought at Phillips, Oxford, auction in a box of drummer's effects.

III 114k Two wooden tubes each containing a reed, one dirtier than the other. The cleaner is rubber stamped PEACOCK and is the higher of the two in pitch; the dirtier is unstamped and is the same pitch as IX 158f. This latter one has been rendered inoperable while investigating how they all work. A smaller wooden cylinder, with a central hole through it, is pushed into the holder, trapping a thin copper blade which acts as a single reed over the hole, similarly to, but more crudely than IX 156. It is probable that the reed on each of these instruments differs in mass, thickness, or shape, so as to differ in tone quality, but that otherwise they are similar in principle. It does not seem sensible to destroy more than one of them, however, to investigate any further. OL 89; ø 22; plug ø 14; hole through plug ø 5.5. [φ 1234/F/18].

IX 158a-f Six wooden bird-imitation single-reed hooters, similar to III 114k, each a tube with a domed top at the proximal end, with the name rubber-stamped on the body: (a) DUNG HILL ROOSTER, (b) BANTAM ROOSTER, (c) Jaybird, (d) BABY CRY, (e) Peacock, (f) REW CACKLE (I have been unable to think of a bird so called). The use of *Jaybird* suggests an American origin for the lower-case rubber stamps, because that name is used there, whereas in Britain the name *Jay* is more common. OL (a) 115, (b) 89, (c) 78.5, (d) 78, (e) 88, (f) 88; ø 22.2, 22, 22.5, 22.5, 22.4, 22.6. They were bought at Phillips, Oxford, auction in a box of drummer's effects.

XI   76   Bicycle horn, the bulb marked © 1989 McDonald's Corp, WM China. Blue plastic horn, orange rubber zoomorphic-head bulb. Metal reed bridled off-centre on a metal shallot produces two pitches, one on squeeze, the second on recovery. OL 140; head ø c. 50; horn ø 48.5. Found in the garden, presumably tossed over from next door. The fitting to attach it to the handle bars is broken; hence perhaps the discard. Probably a give-away or other souvenir from the hamburger chain.

VI   170   Plastic squeaker, France. A thin, oval bulb of orange plastic which, when pressed, sounds a single reed in the neck of the integral horn or spout, producing pitches low on push, higher on suck. The white plastic reed on a metal shallot is held in a plastic sleeve which bridles it off-centre so that each end produces a different pitch. Squeezing the bulb harder also changes the pitch by increasing the speed of the air stream. Presumably a child's toy. OL 160; W 68; th 21. Bought in a street market in Bayonne on a fête day during the IFMC Conference. A second was given to Laurence Picken (his now CUMAE 77.698). [φ 14/1/20].

VIII 166   Squeaker with pink plastic bellows, 9 folds, with a double-ended white plastic single reed on a metal shallot in an orange plastic middle piece, with the bridle off-centre so that each end is tuned to a different pitch, one sounding on push and the other on release. Exponential-flare mauve plastic bell. OL c. 245; bellows ø 67; middle piece ø 28.5; bell 98. Bought at the St. Giles Fair in Oxford; a second was given to the Bate Collection (4058).

XII   142   Crocodile Pipe (so marked). Red plastic mouthpiece, and a yellow plastic body containing a green plastic crocodile. When blown, the crocodile shoots out, its jaws flipping open, revealing a red plastic tongue which forms the spring to open the jaws. The tongue is marked CE Fürth / Made in Germany. The underside of the lower jaw is marked bruder. The butt end of the crocodile's neck contains a white plastic cylinder containing a white plastic double-ended reed and shallot. The reed is bridled off-centre by an internal ring of the cylinder to produce a higher pitch on blow than on draw, but the reed is flexible enough to squeak under high pressure. If one sucks hard, the crocodile pops back into the tube. OL 228; L with crocodile fully extended 290; Ht 32 + ring for holding; W 25. Bought from the Bate Collection, July 1997, probably ex-Hawkin. A second was given to M-Antònia Juan.

XI 284 Bellows-blown single reed. Child's toy, yellow plastic bellows, 25 folds, with a plastic double-ended single reed bridled off-centre in a plastic shallot in a red caterpillar's head with red antennae. OL 253; bellows ø 42.5; head ø 48. Bought in a street market in Palafrugell. Given by Maria Antònia Juan i Nebot.

XI 132a/b Two plastic toys, Taiwan. A plastic tube (a: orange; b: yellow) in which a close-fitting plastic plug can slide up and down as the tube is tipped. One end of the tube has a plain cap, the other a pierced cap to allow air to escape. Inside the plug is a plastic holder which contains a double-ended single reed of white plastic on a metal shallot. The reed is bridled by its holder so that each end is a different length and thus a different pitch, and the reed is light enough that the air speed, as it falls through the tube, affects the pitch and makes the sound warble. An entertaining toy making a rather revolting noise and which demonstrates several acoustical principles. The pierced end of (b) is easily removable for demonstration. OL 405; ext ø 22, int 20; plug ø 19.6, L 29.5. An example was first shown to me by Steve Horenstein. These were bought in a toy shop in Ben Yehuda Street, Jerusalem.

XI 286 Sliding reed. A short version of XI 132 in hammer shape. Green handle, orange hammer head, black caps. The reed is in a holder which slides to and fro in the tube which forms the head of the hammer. OL 202; hammer head L 80, ø 22.5. Bought in a street market in Palafrugell. Given by Maria Antònia Juan i Nebot.

XII 122c Another very similar, marked TAIWAN, but the handles are different shapes and the reed and shallot are different patterns, but again similar to those of XI 132. The caps are immovable on both. Mauve handle, yellow head, orange caps. OL 183; hammer head L 75, ø 22.5. Given to children at a family party, 1 December 1996, and given to me by my grandaughter Kate Roseman, who carefully nabbed musical toys for my collection.

All these hooters and squeakers produce different sounds, and the ability to produce an almost infinite variety of squeaks, squarks, squawks, and hoots is expected of any drummer. The drummer is not only a percussion player, but also the general "effect" man, as well as being expected to play any instrument which other musicians are too exalted or too respectable to play; I have never met a flautist willing to play a nightingale, a cuckoo, or a swannee whistle, for example, all of which are flute variants, and so these are relegated to the drummer who, as a result, often gets a lot more fun than anyone else! See, for instance, Malcolm Arnold's ballet *Sweeney Todd*, with its entertaining nightingale solo.

TRULY IDIOGLOT CYLINDRICAL SINGLE-REED PIPES—422.211

Only a few instruments here are truly idioglot with the reed cut in the head of the instrument itself. The rest, and almost all the geminate instruments of 422.22, have an idioglot reed in a heterozeug mouthpiece.

Instruments of this type, whether single or geminate, go far back into antiquity. The Cairo Museum has, from New Kingdom times, the bodies of two *zummāra* (lacking their zeugs), luted together with wax, not tied with thread (at least, not now tied), but otherwise identical with the body of the modern instrument. Hans Hickmann illustrated both instruments in the *Catalogue Général*, 69837 and 69838, both of them geminate instruments, the former with six pairs of fingerholes, the latter with five, and also in *Ägypten* (Abb. 86), with a wall-painting of a player of Old Kingdom date, c. 2700 B.C. (Abb. 85). It is a reasonable assumption that single instruments of this type are even older, and that those truly idioglot are older still. So long as chromatic music beyond the resources of cross-fingering is not required, and so long as the instruments are not required to overblow beyond the basic range, no improvement is necessary. Thus it is not surprising to find a similar instrument described and illustrated as a *chalumeau* in Mersenne in 1636 and to find others still in use to this day over much of the world. Perhaps the instrument which Mersenne shows was the form of the *chalumeau* that J-C Denner was to improve at the end of the seventeenth century.

Like the shawm, these instruments, especially the geminate ones closest in form to the *zummāra*, are often considered to be indicators of contact with Islam, through trade, conquest, or transmission of culture; despite their inherent simplicity, which could easily lead to independent invention, there seem to be no locations of their use which cannot be explained through such contacts.

The use of a conical bell of wood, coiled leaf, or horn on the end of the cane tube is quite common and does not seem to afford sufficient conicity to change the acoustical character of the instrument, any more than a clarinet bell does. A protective wind-cap or stock, often of the same materials, is also quite common. This avoids saturating the reed in the mouth, and also avoids having to hold such large objects within the mouth cavity for long periods. It is also much easier to "tongue" on a reed cap and thus to make separations between the notes. With the reed pouched wholly in the mouth, this can only be done by closing the glottis, which would interfere with the continuous or circular breathing technique normally used on these instruments as well as on the shawm.

III   132n   Reed pipe made for demonstration. Bamboo with integral idioglot reed. 2 fingerholes; originally there were three but the lower two have joined up because a piece of the tube wall has split away. OL 92; reed L c. 14; bore ø 6.7.

III   134n   A demonstration instrument with a single fingerhole, the vibrating portion of the reed painted green so that it may be distinguished. OL 177; reed L c. 23.5; bore ø 6.6 × 4.7.

VIII   150   Reed pipe, Crete. The upcut reed is integral with the cane pipe, which is stopped by a node at the proximal end, ie truly idioglottal. Reed and 5 burned fingerholes, all ø c. 4.8, on a flattened front surface. Some blue and red decoration; the red has now vanished due to exposure to light. Said to be a practise chanter for the local bagpipe. Smashed longitudinally by the movers when coming to Oxford (one of only two instruments damaged in the move) but successfully glued together. OL 210; reed L c. 29; bore ø 8.3. From Nicholas Shackleton in part-exchange for part of the Mahillon Brussels Catalogue.

XI   98   Reed pipe, Eivissa (Ibiza). The reed truly idioglot and downcut. High th + 6 fingerholes burned in, all ø 4 except the two lowest, 5 × 4.5, 4.6. The base of the reed is lashed with waxed thread as a bridle and to inhibit splitting further down. Attached bell of a horn tip (?goat) into which the pipe is inserted diagonally, which does not seem to be traditional (none of the examples in the Barcelona Museum had such a bell) though all those seen nowadays have a bell either of horn or of a whelk shell. I suspect that this is designed to make them more attractive to tourists. OL 235; horn L 49; reed L c. 40; ext ø 9.6; bore ø inaccessible. Bought from Ramon Pinto Comas, Casa Parramón, Barcelona.

VI   48   Side-blown single-reed pipe, *til'boro*, Zaria, Nigeria. Red leather-covered guinea corn, open at both ends, either of which may be stopped with a finger. 1 thumbhole, knife-cut through the leather cover, at the end furthest from the reed, about 20° off the line of the reed, towards the inside as played. The long, very flexible, truly idioglot reed (*belu* or *beli*), a strip of the cortex about 0.6 thick, which is both blown and sucked, is cut in the side of the tube near one end and has a light cord bridle (*zare*) which is pulled by the player to control it. The pitches produced by blowing and sucking are different, and the flexibility of the reed gives it a tone very similar to that of a free reed. David Ames asked me, on his return from Nigeria, whether I thought that this was a free reed instrument or not, and it was impossible to be certain when listening to the sound on his tapes or from his description. He therefore asked the Gidan Madauchi Ibrahim Bagudu of Zaria to send me an example. It is indeed a side-blown beating reed but with so long and so flexible a reed that the sound is extraordinarily close to that of a free reed such as a mouthorgan. Professor Ames's query was complicated by the fact that players use both inhalation and exhalation, something that occurs with no other single reed instrument known to me, but which is common on free reeds in Asia. I do not know of any side-blown single reeds other than the *til'boro* and its relatives, the *busan karo*, and the *damalgo*, nor of any indigenous African free reeds. The *til'boro* is made only at the time of the guinea-corn harvest and it is made and played by young men for entertainment and pocket money. The leather cover, which is stitched at the back and is decorated in black ink, shows that it is made with some care and trouble, and suggests that the instrument is expected to endure for at least a little time. See David Ames & Anthony King's *Glossary* for full information on this and the next two entries. This was my introduction to the Madauchi, from whom I have obtained a number of instruments of various types over the years. OL 240; reed L 50, Th 0.6, W 3.3; bore ø c. 12.5 or less. On loan to the Bate Collection *(x 4078)*. [φ 6260/11/15-16].

VI   204a/c   Two side-blown reed pipes, *busan karo*, Zaria, Nigeria. In effect a large size *til'boro*, but not leather covered, similar to the *damalgo* but without the gourds and made of a rather lighter reed of the same species. Two internodes long. The nodes at each end are neatly scraped away, the central node presumably knocked out. (a) is red-stained, with a crack covered by transparent adhesive tape, badly cracked at the bottom; most of the red stain has now vanished due to exposure to light. One knife-cut fingerhole near the foot. A bridle of soft string is tied loosely round the head so that it can be moved along the reed and pulled as tight as may be necessary. (b) has slight traces of red stain, and bad cracks at the bottom; cracks at the top are covered by tape (the tape on both was applied, probably by the Madauchi, in Zaria). Bridle of soft string and cotton tape. One burned fingerhole. (c) was given to Bob [no other name is recorded]. (b) is on loan to the Bate Collection *(x 4077)*. Bought per the Madauchi Ibrahim Bagudu, who also provided somewhat impressionistic drawings which are stuck into the ledger catalogue. (a) OL 572; bore ø c. 11, reed L c. 70; fingerhole

100 from the foot. (b) OL 509; bore ø c. 12.5 (irregular) at foot, c. 12 at top; reed L c. 73, th 0.9, W 4.2; fingerhole 105 from foot. (c) was not measured before it was given away. [φ 1237/1].

VI   40a-d   Four side-blown reed pipes, *damalgo*, Zaria, Nigeria. Similar to the *busan karo*, made of two internodes of guinea-corn, but with a spherical gourd over the proximal end and another gourd over the foot; covered from immediately after the reed to the foot with red leather stitched at the back, with black ink decoration and two prominent leather tassels. A fingerhole burned through the leather cover near the distal end is stopped with the left thumb. The lower gourd is fairly firmly fixed between the swelling of the lower node and the end of the leather sleeve. The upper gourd of (a) is partly broken, that of (b) is intact; the lower gourd of each has a round hole cut in it approximately 45° from the line of the bore so that it can be stopped by the palm of the hand when the thumb is over the fingerhole. The reed bridle is of hard string. (b) is on loan to the Bate Collection *(x 4076)*; (d) was given to Laurence Picken (now CUMAE 77. 516). The location of (c) is unknown. Bought per the Madauchi Ibrahim Bagudu. (a) OL c. 590; body L c. 480; bore ø c. 14.5; reed L c. 75; hand hole ø on lower gourd c. 30 × 40. b) OL c. 591; body L c. 542; bore ø c. 17; reed L c. 70, th 0.9, W 4.9; hand hole ø 30.5 × 38.5. [φ 6260/2/13-21].

IV   60   Plastic truly idioglot clarinet, PEDIWEST, MADE IN ENGLAND, REGD. DES. PROV. PAT. 551/68, c. 1970. High th ø 5.5 + 7 fingerholes ø 4, 6, 6, 6.3, 5.4, 6.6, 6.7, slightly raised with integral collars, the uppermost very small, a rear vent ø 5.2 in the bell. A child's keyless *chalumeau*. Made in a mould in two pieces, front and back, the reed integral with the back and the shallot integral with the front. An integral decorative raised ring at the base of the mouthpiece and at the root of the bell. Some accidental red staining on the white plastic, probably from a rotted balloon bagpipe (for which see below) which it may have been touching. Similar in effect to the Danish wooden instrument reported by

Mette Müller, though that is a folk instrument, rather than a child's. Mette Müller is definite that the *skalmeje* is a back-formation from the clarinet, as are the Pediwest here, the German schools clarinets (I 166), the Norwegian Meråker clarinets (XI 78), and the Hawaiian xaphoon (XII 158) below, and not an ancestor. OL 328; bore ø 11.1; bell ø 37; reed L 22.5, W 11.9; pitch C. On loan to the Bate Collection *(x 4075)*. [φ 1234/B/1-2].

IDIOGLOT/HETEROZEUG
CYLINDRICAL SINGLE REEDS—422.211

XI   258a   Cylindrical piece of aluminium tubing, made by JM for demonstration. Accepts a single reed made from a goose quill and an oboe reed staple. It is similar in length to a stepped shawm made of three segments of aluminium tubing inserted into each other (XI 258b in 422.212 below), and the pair was constructed to show the different effects of cylindrical and conical reed-driven bores, described above, irrespective of the type of reed. The cylindrical example overblows to the twelfth with either reed, and the conical to the octave. I have not yet succeeded in making a free reed of the correct size to drive these air columns. OL 288, bore ø 7.1.

IX   226   Reed pipe, Sunda, West Java. Heterozeug mouthpiece with idioglot downcut reed inserted into a reed pipe with 4 knife-cut fingerholes, all ø c. 5. The mouthpiece is very firmly fixed in the body and has therefore not been removed; it appears to be cut off obliquely, like that of XI 114, but if so with the longest part at the front, proper with the reed, rather than at the side. Bought from Ganesha, run by Marten Timmer, a one-time importer of Indonesian artefacts and records. OL 169; body L 111; bore ø 7.7; mouthpiece L ? (projecting 57.5); reed L c. 22; bore ø ? because not extricable.

XI   114   Reed pipe *bansi*, Padang, West Sumatra. Reed tube with four fingerholes, all ø c. 6.5, burned in, with heterozeug mouthpiece with idioglot downcut reed inserted into one end. The mouthpiece is a cane tube, blocked by a pith plug at the proximal end. The distal end of the mouthpiece is cut off obliquely at 90° to the reed and inserted into the tube so that the oblique end fits beside the uppermost fingerhole. Similar to IX 226 but wider in bore and longer. Given by Vafa Taghasi, a child who had bought several out there. OL 189; body L 130; bore ø 9.3; mouthpiece L 8-9.25; bore ø 6.7; reed L c. 24.

IX   100   Reed pipe, bagless chanter, Hungary. Elderwood pipe with a heterozeug mouthpiece with idioglot downcut reed inserted. High th + 6 knife-cut fingerholes left very rough with no attempt to even them out. The mouthpiece is lapped with thread to hold it in position and this was not disturbed. Given by Tony Bingham, 24 December 1984, who had bought it from a man at a folk fair, who was making such pipes while people watched. OL 229; L without reed 195; bore ø at foot 8.5; reed L c. 20, W 4.3. On loan to the Bate Collection (*x 4087*).

V   90a/b   Two reed pipes, India. Only the larger (a) has been found (March 1997); some duplicate instruments have been given to colleagues over the years, and sometimes this has not been recorded. Each with a heterozeug mouthpiece with an idioglot downcut reed inserted into the instrument, the mouthpiece contained in a bamboo windcap. Each with 3 knife-cut fingerholes: (a) ø 7.5 × 5.5, 7.5 × 5.5, 6 × 5.5. They are different lengths, a) the longer and b) the shorter, and are not intended to be used together. Decorated with red, blue, and gold paper. Bought from Cargo, Cleveland, Ohio, 1970. OL 202 but variable for the mouthpiece is held in place by a sliver of bamboo as a wedge and it can be slid in and out; body L 143, bore ø 8.4; mouthpiece L 92, bore ø 6.2; windcap L 68, bore ø 13.4; reed L c. 30. [φ 6260 /8/6].

XII   86a-c   Three reed pipes, *Péschtschiki* or *Schaleika* of light cane and one horn bell, Belgorod people, Afanasieroka Village, Alekscierd Region, South Russia. Although they were given as a group, all given by Vyacheslav Shourov during the

ESEM Seminar in Rotterdam, 1995, with a single name and source, these appear to be three quite different instruments. a and b have a heterozeug mouthpiece with an idioglot downcut reed. The proximal end of the mouthpieces is not stopped; either a pith plug has fallen out or more probably the player's tongue is used to stop the end. Both have rectangular knife-cut fingerholes, (a) with 5 and (b) with 6.

a) is wider in bore than b), made of a slightly thicker cane, has differently shaped fingerholes, 9.7 × 5.4, rectangular but with slightly rounded ends, and has a cowhorn bell. Its mouthpiece is wrapped with green plastic(?) tape to make it fit the body (sufficiently tightly that it could not be removed), and the distal end of the body, which is cut off obliquely so that the bore faces forward within the bell, is lapped with similar tape to fit the bell. The proximal end of the body is cut off in an upward-pointing V. The downcut reed may be bridled with black thread (a tag projects from underneath the tape). The bell is a cow horn with a triangular hole cut in the side just at the end of the hollow to accept the pipe; the end, which faces forward in use, is neatly cut in 30 points. OL c. 233; L without bell 179; body L 144, bore ø 6.5; mouthpiece L ? (projecting 40), bore ø? because not extricable; bell ø 43.6 × 47.7; reed L 25.

b) has a heterozeug mouthpiece lapped with paper which is not held securely; each end of the body is cut off flat and there may have been no bell. The downcut idioglot reed is bridled with thread which is easily movable. The six fingerholes are rectangular, from 10 to 12.5 × 4.5. The body is badly cracked. OL c. 265; body L 216, bore ø c. 6; mouthpiece L 108, bore ø 5.5; reed L c. 32.

c) is quite different. The 4 fingerholes are approximately round and are knife-haggled, ø 4.2 × 4.8, 4 × 5, 3.8 × 5.5, 4.5 × 6.3. The proximal end is cut off obliquely, longest at the front, and there is a truly idioglot downcut reed. This instrument should be in the previous section, that for the truly idioglot. However, because these all came together from Dr. Shourov, and also because it is only guess work that allocates the horn bell to (a), it seems best to keep them together. The end is not plugged and is stopped with the tongue, which is why it is obliquely cut. The distal end is cut off flat. OL 160; reed L c. 32; bore ø 7.7.

VII   122   Hornpipe, *pibcorn*, Philip Bate, London. Reconstruction of the ancient Welsh instrument, based on the surviving example belonging to the Society of Antiquaries of London, of which Philip Bate is also a Fellow, and which is now deposited in the Museum of Welsh Life at St. Fagan's. Horn reed cap and horn bell of cow horn, the reed cap plain, the bell with the traditional jaw-shape cut-out and dentation decoration; single, cylindrical-bore, wooden pipe stained black with high thumb + 6 finger-holes, all ø c. 3.2, and a cork-lapped male tenon on each end to fit into the horns, each of which has a brass ferrule to protect the socket. The heterozeug straw mouthpiece, stopped at the top with red sealing wax, with a downcut reed (as for a Northumbrian bagpipe) is not properly tuned, for which PATB apologised—he had not succeeded in doing so. It is firmly fixed into a cork-lined socket and could not be removed without risk of breakage. Made as a gift for me. Another is in the Bate Collection (4059). OL 418; body L (+9) 144 (+12), bore ø 7.1; reed cap L 104, bell L 179; mouthpiece L ?; reed L c. 33. [φ 1247 and 1248].

SETS OF IDIOGLOT CYLINDRICAL SINGLE REEDS—422.22

The use of the geminate chanter, two parallel pipes, either two distinct pipes, normally fixed together, or two bores drilled in one piece of wood, both with fingerholes, which are fingered across both pipes (i.e., with each finger covering two holes side by side, one on each pipe), is widespread, both with reedpipes and flutes, and of high antiquity. The main reason for the use of geminate pipes seems to be that if the pipes are tuned just off the unison, the sound of each reinforces the other, with the resulting beats between the two pitches adding further interest to the sound. Two pitches which are almost, but not quite, in unison will beat or throb, the number of beats per second being the number of vibrations (Hz) that separate them. Thus the closer they come to a true unison, the slower the throb, and the more distant the faster. A difference of five or six Hz will produce a fairly normal vibrato, whereas ten or a dozen will produce the howl which earlier generations, with more sensitive ears than ours, and a more precise tuning system than our generalised Equal Temperament, castigated as the wolf, produced by playing a G♯ instead of an A♭.

One question with the *zummāra*-type instruments is why their stepped cone construction (normally a mouthpiece or *zeugos*, stepped into a slightly wider intermediate section or middle piece, which, in turn, is stepped into the slightly wider body) does not render the instrument acoustically conical. Anthony Baines suggested, in conversation, that this may be because the *zeug* is closed by a node in the cane at the upper end, but this is not a valid reason, for the quill single reed, on a conical bore, as on the Hungarian shawm referred to by Bálint Sárosi, overblows octaves. So does the quill single reed on the aluminium stepped cone, XI 258b. This also eliminates the possible reason that the cane sections of the *zummāra* are too wide in bore and insufficiently different in diameter to be effective as a stepped cone, for certainly the *zummāra's* mouthpiece and middle piece are much wider in bore, proportionate to their length, than the staple and initial steps of the Mediterranean shawm's fork. However, the bores and thicknesses of XI 258b are little different from those of the *zummāra*, and XI 258b is effectively conical. Certainly proportionate bore diameter is important; a cylindrical tube which will accept a modern oboe staple becomes, when long enough in proportion to its diameter, effectively conical, as experiment will show, overblowing octaves not twelfths. Presumably this is why a seven-foot-six long hosepipe-trumpet functions as a trumpet, overblowing all the harmonics of the D fundamental despite its cylindricity, and for that matter why a proper natural trumpet or a trombone, even extended to seventh position, behave as though they were conical even though they are cylindrical save for the bell. The clarinet's bell flare, which begins around the f/c′ hole is longer, proportionately to its length, than a trombone's, but the clarinet's bore is much wider, in relation to its length, than a trombone's. Which does, however, leave the question of why a contrabass clarinet (even more, the unique octobass) still behaves cylindrically, overblowing twelfths, even though its proportions are much closer to those of the reed and cylindrical tube noted above. There is much that we do not yet know about acoustics.

XII 164 Geminate pipes, *qoshnai*, Horesm, Uzbekistan. Down-cut, truly idioglot-idiozeug reeds. 7 rectangular fingerholes, all approximate "ø" 5.5 or 6 × 4.5; each fingerhole is in the centre of a knife-cut "field" about 17 long, except the uppermost, which has only the part of the field below the hole. The two pipes linked only by a twined cord 405 long, tied round each pipe immediately below the base of the reed and tied to a tassel at midpoint, and held divergently but so that each finger can, as usual with geminate pipes, cover a pair of fingerholes, one on each pipe. The reed comes from the Pandjkent mountain area in Tadjikistan, said to be the only area in which it grows. The Vertkov *Atlas* shows it from Uzbekistan (581) and, slightly differently, from Tadjikistan (629). *Qosh* = double; *nai* = flute. OL 235 and 233; ø 7.8 and 7.1, c. 12 ext; reed L c. 51 and 50. Brought specially from Uzbekistan and given by Razia Soultanova, December 1997.

XI 96 Geminate reed-pipe of cane, *Reclam de Xeremia*, Eivissa. Similar to a *zummāra* but the reeds are truly idioglot-idiozeug and are downcut. Four fingerholes burned in each pipe, ø L: 5, 5, 4.6, 4; R: 4.5, 4.3, 4, 4.2, with other burned decoration. The right-hand pipe is longer than the left. The pipes are lashed together with yellow thread. A modern instrument, rather wider in bore and coarser than those in the Barcelona Museum. Bought from Ramon Pinto Comas, Casa Parramón, Barcelona. OL 200; left pipe L 186; bore ø rh 8, lh 7; reed L c. 42.

I 150a Geminate reed-pipe, *zummāra*, Egypt. Bamboo tubes held together with tarred twine; 6 circular fingerholes in each, very neatly knife-cut (if they were burned, all traces of charring have been removed), all ø c. 6.8. Heterozeug mouthpieces with upcut idioglot reeds. Two spare mouthpieces are attached with a long twine, as are the inserted mouthpieces. Bought in Egypt while stationed in the Canal Zone with the army in 1948; this was when I first became interested in the musics of other cultures, hearing Egyptian music on the loudspeakers in the streets of Port Said, and being introduced to Hans Hickmann by the staff of the Institut Fouad Premier de Musique Arabe, in search for further information, while on leave in Cairo. This and I 148a must also be the first instruments in this collection. OL 315; body L 218 and 220 (all first left and then right); middle piece L 51 and 51; zeug 44 and 41; reed L c. 15 and 16 (the end cut on a slant), W 7 & 5.7; body bore ø 11 and 10.4 (mouthpieces not removed so middle piece bore not measured). On loan to the Bate Collection *(x 4084)*. [φ 3181/40; b/w sl; 3021/34 is a detail of the mouthpieces].

I   150b   Geminate reed-pipe, *zummāra*, perhaps Arabia—but Anthony Baines *(Bagpipes)* illustrates an identical instrument (fig. 12c, p. 34) from the Pitt Rivers Museum (1948.3.3) which is said to have come from Bethlehem. Conical bone tubes, presumably crane or eagle, held together with soldered metal bands at top and bottom (non-responsive to a magnet so perhaps brass); a strip of metal, lying between the bones, joins them at the back, with a soldered-on metal ring below the top band to which the very short cane middle pieces, held together with tarred twine, are tied. Six drilled fingerholes in each tube, all ø c. 5.5. Heterozeug mouthpieces with upcut idioglot reeds; some hair remains under the left reed. Ring and dot incised and black-filled decoration, with two parallel lines above and below each fingerhole, with four rings in two pairs between each (i.e., fingerhole, 2 lines, 4 rings, 2 lines, fingerhole), and eleven rings between the lowest fingerhole and the foot (5 pairs with a single central above). All beautifully made and very light weight. OL 264 and 266 (L and R); bodyL 188 and 188; middle piece L 25 and 28; zeug L 51 and 51; reed L c. 28 (the ends cut on a slant), W 5.5 and 6.5; bore ø at foot 14.2 × 12 (triangular) on both. On loan to the Bate Collection *(x 4069)*. [φ 3181/40; b/w sl].

I   150c   Geminate reed-pipe, *zummāra*, Bethlehem. Cane tubes, 5 fingerholes, burned and then knife-cut, in each, ø L: 7, 6.5,

6.3, 6.2, 6.3; R: 7, 6.5, 6.5, 6, 6. The tubes are held together insecurely by tarred twine. Left-hand middle piece is cracked and secured with transparent adhesive tape. Heterozeug mouthpieces with upcut idiglot reeds. Tourist instrument bought from Bethlehem Bible Lands. OL 270; body (L and R) L 163 and 160, bore ø 9.7 and 10; middle piece L 53 and 57, bore ø 8.2 and 8.8; mouthpiece L 64 and 67; reed L c. 26 and c. 22. [φ 1234/I/31].

IV   226   Geminate reed-pipe, *zummāra*, Jerusalem. Cane tubes, 6 fingerholes burned and then knife-cut in each, ø L: 6, 5.7, 5.7, 5.7, 6.6, 6.7; R: 6, 6.4, 6.2, 6.5, 6.7, 6.5. No middle joint; the heterozeug mouthpieces with upcut idioglot reeds go straight into the body. Held together with black-waxed string. Quite roughly made and clearly a tourist instrument. Given by Vladimir Prager. OL 315; body L 249, ø top 10.6, bottom 9; mouthpiece L 79.5 and 81.8, ø 8.4; reed L c. 29 [φ1234/Q/1-2].

XII   134   Geminate reed-pipe, *zummāra*, origin unknown. Cane tubes, 6 fingerholes quite roughly knife-cut in each, ø L: 7, 6.8, 6, 6.6, 6.4, 6.6; R: 6.5, 6.8, 7, 5.5, 6.5, 6.5. Otherwise much better quality than the two previous instruments but both up-cut reeds are broken off the heterozeug mouthpieces. The sections are lashed with tarred twine longitudinally as well as to each other, so that the middle pieces cannot be removed. Source unknown; found while preparing this catalogue. OL 379; body L 243, bore ø c. 10; middle piece exposed L 91, bore ø 7.5; mouthpiece L 47; reed window L c. 16.5 & 15.

VIII   122a-c   Three geminate reed-pipes, *zummāra*. Held together with string and yellow wax. Cane tubes, 6 fingerholes burned in each, all ø c. 5.7. Bought as modern playing instruments from a pedlar at the source of the Jordan. (b) not found. (c) on loan to the Bate Collection *(x 4070)*, fingerholes all ø c. 5.5. (a) OL 376; L with out mouthpieces 328; body L 273, bore ø at foot 8.8 and 8.5; middle piece L c. 55, bore ø 7.3 and 7.5; mouthpieces L 57 and 59, reed L c. 20 and 21, ø 5.5 and 6. (c) OL 369; L without mouthpieces 319; body L

c. 259; middle piece L c. 60; mouthpiece L 49; reed L c. 22 and 20, W 4.9 and 5.2.

VI   160   Geminate hornpipe, *alboka*, Basque, Spain. Horn reedcap, wooden yoke with two heart-shaped cutouts, geminate pipes, and horn bell with one hole in each side of the bell, opposite each other (i.e., drilled straight through). Finger-holes burned in, 5 in the left-hand pipe, 3 in the right-hand, all ø c. 5.8. A twisted wire through a small frontal hole in the bell holds a horn ring, octagonal externally, round internally. The end of the bell has scalloped indentations, neat but quite wide, c. 8.5 from peak to peak. The bell horn seems held to the yoke only by wax; the mouth horn has two small nails on each side as well as wax, presumably because it is subjected to pressure when in use. The pipes are luted together with wax and the heterozeug mouthpieces are embedded in wax (the left hand one is loose and was extracted and measured). Idioglot reeds are downcut, bridled with white thread; each has a blob of tuning wax near the tip. The instrument is held with the thumbs below the wood, not through the holes in the yoke, and is played with circular breathing. This is the most important of the Basque instruments, and the one which they regard as a ritual instrument. Bought in Bayonne from Jean Sarrazin, one of a group of Basque nationalists whom I met while there for the IFMC Conference in 1973. OL 307; L pipes between the horns c. 112; mouth horn L c. 100, ø 35.3; bell L c. 160, ø 48.7 × 50.7; mouthpiece L 47; reed L 24, W 5.3; yoke L below horns 98.5, depth below pipes 56. On loan to the Bate Collection *(x 4074)*. [φ 14/1/17-19].

XII   24   Geminate hornpipe, *alboka*, Leon Bilbao, Basque Spain. Neatly made, the yoke with two heart-shaped cut-outs, and initials LB along with scroll patterns. The horn bell with three holes on each side (small, larger, small) and very fine dentations on the edge. Both the horns are pinned to the yoke with 2 small nails on each side; the canes are luted to it and to the horns with beeswax. A horn octagonal ring attached to the bell by a copper wire holds a chain which goes to the front cut-out (presumably a similar chain is missing from the previous instrument). Heterozeug mouthpieces embedded in wax, with idioglot downcut reeds, are bridled with white thread and are well and properly tuned to produce beating unisons; for this reason they were not disturbed even though this prevented detailed measurement (this can be done in the future when it is necessary to remove the mouthpieces for other reasons). Five burned fingerholes in the left-hand pipe; 3 in the right-hand parallel with the lowest three in the left, all ø 5. A better-made instrument than VI 160. Given by Sabin Bikandi Belandia, with an LP played by the maker in exchange for some books. OL 280; pipe L between horns 113; mouth horn L 87; bell horn L 160, ø 45 × 50; yoke L below horns 10; yoke depth 64.

III   36   Geminate hornpipe, *zukra*, Tunisia. Cane pipes, 5 fingerholes in each, all ø c. 6, burned and knife cut, each pipe with its own horn bell. A stitched red leather sleeve covers the joint between the heterozeug mouthpieces and the body, covering almost the whole of the middle pieces, and a black sleeve covers the joint between the bodies and the bells. The mouthpieces with idioglot reeds fit fairly loosely but are attached with twine (which is not tarred). There is no reedcap. See also the bagpipe V 258 which has the same name and is the same instrument blown through a bag. Bought from Tradewinds, Mere. OL c. 343; body L c. 160, middlepiece L c. 33; mouthpiece L 48 and 46; reed L 32, W c. 6.2; bell ø 49 × 45 and 52 × 49.5 On loan to the Bate Collection *(x 4073)*. [φ 1234/J/29-30; b/w sl].

IX   54   Geminate pipes, *mišnice* or *diple*, Istra, North Croatia. Described by Anthony Baines (*Bagpipes*, fig. 39, p. 73) as a bagless chanter. Two bores burned in a single piece of wood with heterozeug mouthpieces with downcut reeds, in a separate wooden stock, with some incised decoration. The stock, which is here used as a windcap, is similar to those of bagpipes in the same area, still with a deep groove at the upper edge as though for tying into a bag. Three fingerholes in the left hand pipe near the foot, 5 in the right, all ø 4.2, 2 near the foot parallel with the two lowest on the left, then a gap so that there is no hole opposite the uppermost in the left, and then 3 higher. The front surface is deeply scalloped, with a fingerhole at the bottom of each recess. Each pipe has a lateral vent, ø c. 3, above the lowest fingerhole. All the holes, and the bores, are burned, and all the holes slope sharply downwards from the bore to the surface. This is the normal type of *diple* with the two pipes carved from one piece of wood. Given by Ankica Petrovic. OL 193; body L 153; windcap L 52; mouthpiece L 38.8, reed L c. 21; bore ø 6.3; body W 25.5, Th 14.

IX   56   Double pipes, *roženice* (small horn) or *diple*, Istra, North Croatia. With divergent boxwood pipes, conical bore, in a wooden stock. Much decorative turning. Four fingerholes in the right-hand pipe, 3 in the left-hand, all ø c. 3.6. Only the right-hand pipe was removable without using excessive pressure, and the heterozeug mouthpiece of that pipe was firmly fixed. Downcut idioglot reeds. Given by Ankica Petrovic. OL 210; body L 170; windcap L 60; mouthpiece L ?; reed L c. 25; bore ø top c. 6.4, bottom c. 12 and then flared to c. 32.

I   148a   Double pipe, *arghūl*, Egypt. Small size. Mouthpieces and bodies only; there are no middle pieces. The chanter (right-hand pipe) has 6 knife-cut fingerholes all ø c. 5.8; the drone has a mark parallel with each hole. Only one extension to the drone survives, and does not in fact belong to this instrument; it is slightly too narrow to fit; it has tarred twine at the end which was attached to the next extension now missing. Bought in Egypt while stationed in the Canal Zone with the army in 1948 as I 150a above. OL 304; chanter L 244; drone body L 270; chanter body L 209; drone extension L 194; mouthpiece L 33 and 37 (but amount of correct insertion is uncertain); reed L c. 19 and 20, W 4.8 and 5.2. On loan to the Bate Collection (*x 4085*). [φ 1234/E/24; 3181/1].

I   148b   Double pipe, *arghūl*, Egypt. Large size. The chanter (right-hand pipe) has 7 knife-cut fingerholes, ø varying from 7 to

9, 3 of them quite neat and the others quite rough, + 2 vents. The drone has two extensions. However, the tenons and sockets of the drone and the extensions do not match coherently, even though each is attached with tarred twine; the end of the fixed drone is shaved down to form a male tenon, the short first extension begins with a similar male tenon and ends with a female internal chamfer, and the long second extension begins with a similar male tenon and ends with a similar female chamfer, suggesting that there is a third extension missing; there are traces of tar where twine has been round that end, as though to attach it to a further piece. Even if the attachment cords have been shifted, so that the first extension should be the other way round, while its female chamfer would fit over the male tenon of the fixed drone, one would still be left with its male tenon confronting the male tenon of the second extension. It is very problematic working out just how, and whether, this instrument and the extensions link up. With two spare heterozeug mouthpieces attached. Bought from Michael Morrow. OL 715; chanter L 567; drone body and middle piece 665; chanter body and middle piece 516; drone body 565; chanter body 410; OL with short extension c. 840, with both c. 1400; mouthpiece L 52 and 51; reed L 24.4 and 26, W 7.4 and 7.7, ø 11.6 and 11.4; spare reeds L 29.2 and 29.4, W 7.6 and 7.4, ø 29 and 25; middle piece ø 10.9 and 10.5; drone foot ø 15. On loan to the Bate Collection *(x 4071)*. [φ 1234/E/23; b/w sl].

I   146a   Double pipe, *pūngī*, India. Brown gourd wind chamber with 6 patches of beeswax on the front surface which have indentations where small metal decorations were inserted, all but two of which are missing. Two black wooden pipes with drilled bores are held in with beeswax. Right-hand chanter has 6 drilled fingerholes ø 4.5, 5, 4.5, 4.7, 4.5, 4.3; left-hand pipe is a drone. Reed type is unknown because it is inaccessible within the gourd, though it is likely to be downcut, from comparison with the following, but certainly with a heterozeug mouthpiece. Although this type of instrument is best known abroad as a snake charmer's pipe, in India they are regarded as normal musical instruments and are used for all purposes. Bought at the Do-it-Yourself Exhibition, Olympia. OL 320; exposed pipe L 133, bore ø 7.7; gourd ø c. 110. [φ 5868/40; b/w sl].

I   146b   Double pipe, *pūngī*, India. Coconut shell wind chamber. Bamboo pipes, chanter with 6 fingerholes, turned wood mouthpipe, originally held together with wax, but subsequently disintegrated. Downcut reeds. Decorated with seeds and shells stuck to the body with wax. Given to Laurence Picken in 1970, before any measurements were taken, so that he could have a disintegrated instrument for demonstration; now CUMAE 77.552. [φ 3181/2; disintegrated 1234/J/31-32 & 1234/L/1-2].

VI   180   Double pipe, *pūngī*, Calcutta, India. Coconut wind chamber, turned wooden mouthpipe. Red-stained bamboo pipes, the right-hand chanter with th + 7 burned fingerholes, all ø c. 6, the lowest offset to the right, the left-hand drone with 2 thumbholes for the right (lower) thumb to allow a change of drone, the upper hole half blocked with shellac to tune it. The two pipes were held together at the foot with shellac, now broken, and held into the wind chamber with beeswax, also now broken. The red-stained wooden mouthpipe is still held insecurely with wax and shellac. Decorated with a necklet of white and green glass beads round the coconut and red tassels with 5 red beads at the distal end of the pipes. Given by Sreenata Mitra. OL c. 420; chanter L 244, bore ø 8; the heterozeug mouthpiece with downcut reed is held into the chanter with shellac; the drone prefers not to come out of the gourd and is unmeasured but is presumably similar. [φ 14/8/10-11].

IV   244   Double pipe, *pūngī*, India. Coconut wind chamber. Wooden pipes. Chanter with th + 7 burned fingerholes. Brown stained. Disassembled so that the heterozeug mouthpieces with down-cut reeds may be seen. The chanter mouthpiece is cut off on a slant to fit the thumbhole. Given in Paris. OL c. 465; pipe L 217; chanter bore ø 9, drone 9.5; chanter mouthpiece projects 43.3, drone 62.3; chanter reed L 35, W 5.4, drone 25, 4.4; coconut L c. 110, ø c. 84; mouthpipe L c. 155. On loan to the Bate Collection (*x 4089*). [φ 1234/Z/2-3].

VIII 42 Double pipe, *pūngī*, India. Heavy wooden wind chamber with carved decoration of flowers and so forth, very well done, and wooden pipes. Th + 6 fingerholes, all bushed with plastic rings, all ø c. 3.5 in righthand pipe, the left a drone. Heterozeug mouthpieces with down-cut reeds, the chanter reed broken off. The almost equidistant spacing of the fingerholes is unusual, with the highest close to the upper end and the lowest close to the foot, but this is clearly deliberate because the chanter reed is shaped to clear the uppermost hole. The pipes were joined at the foot by a thin copper wire, now missing. From the World of Islam Exhibition. The pipes alone were bought at Sotheby's, 20/11/80, lot 193, catalogued as Persian and in the same lot as the *balaban*, VIII 40. The wooden "gourd" appeared a year later in the sale 5/11/81 (lot 55) and, when purchased, was catalogued here as VIII 202 (qv); only later was it recognised that the two belonged together. OL c. 398; chanter body L 224; drone body L 225, with mouthpiece 273, reed L 30, W 4.3; chanter bore ø 8.5, drone 7; "gourd" L 180, ø 110, wood thickness where pipes enter c. 12.5. On loan to the Bate Collection (*x 4068*). [φ 1253/33-34 as bought, i.e., pipes only].

VII 158 Triple pipe, *pūngī*, India. Yellow gourd wind chamber with yellow beads in snake patterns embedded in black wax as decoration. Chanter of light reed with 7 fingerholes with a drone of the same material on each side of it. Wooden mouthpipe. All loosely held together with black wax, much of which, including the decoration, is breaking away; it was too fragile to take detailed measurements. Tartan ribbon from the mouthpipe to the distal end. Bought in Islington. OL c. 275; chanter bore ø 6. [φ 1249].

VIII 202a/b Two *pūngī* gourds, India. (a) of coconut shell painted reddish black, the yellow-painted bamboo mouthpipe with red-painted proximal end held in with wax and shellac. Much the most firmly fixed of all the *pūngī* mouthpipes—a pity that the pipes have disappeared. OL 180. (b) is heavily and ornately carved wood shaped as a gourd, with two holes drilled for the pipes, which are not quite proper to the mouthpipe, so that when played, with the "gourd" facing outwards, the pipes project downwards rather than outwards. The holes were recognised to be an exact fit for the pipes of VIII 42 (*supra*), to which this wind-chamber is now assigned. It was purely by chance that I bought both lots and was able to reassemble the instrument, because this lot (lot 55) attracted no bids at Sotheby's auction 5/11/81, and I bought it after the sale. It included also the "Highland" bagpipe chanter IV 204, a 2-string *ektar*, and a *gopi yantra*. (b) "gourd" L 180, ø 110, wood thickness where pipes enter c. 12.5. (b) is on loan to the Bate Collection as part of VIII 42 *(x 4068)*.

BAGPIPES

I   200a/d Four balloon bagpipes, Italy. Children's Christmas toy, used at Advent. Chanter with 5 square knife-cut fingerholes (a), 4 fingerholes (b/c), each with a single drone. All the balloons, which were pink or light brown, have now perished. (d) was given to the Pitt Rivers Museum. Gifts from my sister Jennifer. Only (a) could be found when compiling this catalogue, with the mouthpipe and stock of either (b) or (c). Mouthpipe L 98, bore ø 11; chanter and stock L 304, bore ø 12.3, heterozeug mouthpiece L 87, upcut reed L 47.5; drone and stock L 226, bore ø 10. The drone was not removed from its stock, and therefore the mouthpiece and reed not examined, so as not to disturb the original newspaper lapping. [φ (a) 5868/2; b/w sl; b and c 1234/Y/39].

The bagpipe is the traditional Christmas instrument in Italy, not only because pipers come to the cities from the Abruzzi with their *zampogna* and *ciaramella* (the *Pifa* which Handel imitated in the "Pastoral Symphony"

in his *Messiah*), but because almost every Italian painting of the Annuncia-
tion to the Shepherds includes a bagpiper, as do the assemblages of crib figures in churches and other folk carvings.

VIII   6   Balloon bagpipe, Italy. Chanter with 6 rectangular knife-
cut fingerholes, marked ROMA in felt pen, single drone.
Child's Christmas toy. Dark red balloon now perished but
cementing all together so that some parts were not examined. Also from Jennifer. Mouthpipe L 95, bore ø 7.9;
chanter and stock L 307, bore ø 9.1; drone and stock L 231,
bore ø 7.7. [φ 1248, the bag already perished].

V   258   Bagpipe, *zukra*, Tunisia. Geminate pipes, each with a separate horn bell, 5 burned fingerholes in each, all ø c. 6.3 with
two burned dots between each fingerhole and other burned
dots down the outer sides. The horn bells each have a hole
on what would be the frontal side in use (the underside at
rest). The bells are held to the pipes with thick thread covered by badly deteriorated transparent adhesive tape, covered by a black leather sleeve, and by better cord which
passes through a hole into the pipe stock. The pipes fit
neatly into the stock. Sheep- or goatskin bag, the forelegs
plugged with wooden pegs, a wooden disc as a pipe stock
tied into the neck; the back and back legs are tied off in a
bundle. The heterozeug mouthpieces with idioglot downcut reeds are loose in the chanters and keep falling out into
the bag, which means untying the cord round the neck to
remove the stock and fish them out. By the time they are
replaced, the stock reinserted and all tied up again, they
have usually fallen out again into the bag. The copper
mouthpipe, without a non-return valve (the player's tongue
is used instead), is held by wax into a turned wooden block.
With 2 spare mouthpieces. Very similar to the Tunisian
geminate pipe III 36 of the same name, save that this is
blown through the bag and the other by mouth, evidence
that the bag is simply a labour-saving device, to avoid
circular breathing. Bought in a Tunisian restaurant in Amsterdam, to which Arthur Briegleb and I were taken by
Sylvia Broere-Moore and Bernhard Broere during the

midwinterhoorn expedition in 1974 (cf *GSJ* XXVIII). OL from the end of the bag to the ends of the horns c. 665; pipe L between stock and horns c. 110; bell ø 43.4 × 35.6 and 44.4 × 34.6. On loan to the Bate Collection *(x 4060)* until the similar instrument which John Burton presented to the Bate is cleaned up enough to display. [φ 6260/11/21].

HETEROGLOT CYLINDRICAL SINGLE REEDS—422.211

VIII 26 Reed *rozhok*, Anatoly Zajaruzny, Kiev, Ukraine. Wooden tube with burned dedication: TO DEAR JEREMY WITH BEST WISHES / FROM YOUR ANATOLY ~ KIEV ~ USSR ~ 1979, with leaves and flowers, and each of the high thumbhole (ø 4) and 6 fingerholes (all ø c. 5) is surrounded by a flower head, all in very fine and neat pyrography. With a horn bell ending in 7 rounded points, each with 9 small holes drilled in it, and one hole at the apex of the V between each point; the body appears to be glued into the bell. The thin, narrowly rectangular cane heteroglot reed is tied on to a black, turned plastic mouthpiece, but traditional models were idioglot. The reed was better undisturbed so the window was not measured. The wooden mouthpiece cap is marked: ZAJARUZNY / KIEV in Cyrillic characters, with more flowers, and is held to the body with a thin red leather cord, and to the end of the bell with a soft leather cord made of black, orange, and red strands with orange, red, black, orange, red, leather tassels. Made as a gift for me; I had asked the maker whether the cornett-type rozhok were obtainable, but this, which is almost equally interesting, is what arrived. OL with cap c. 380; mouthpiece L 44.5 (+10 ø 6); body L 169; bore ø 8.2; bell L c. 155 to point, 125 to valley between points, ø 61.5 × 65. On loan to the Bate Collection *(x 4072)*. [φ 1252/0-1].

VIII 178 "Clarinet," China. Straight bamboo tube, red-painted, the integral clarinet mouthpiece at the upper end formed from some sort of mastic, the end now slightly chipped, with a ligature of bent, flat, ferrous metal, holding a reed cut from bamboo, in size much that of a narrow E♭ reed, with a sharp step to a flat blade with no central spine. The long lay is knife cut in the wall of the bamboo; the window is rectangular with sharp corners. High th ø 8.5 + 6 fingerholes ø 8.3, 9.2, 9.2, 8.3, 10.2, 9.2. From the E. O. Pogson Collection. Bought at Sotheby's, 5/11/91, part of lot 47, which was bought by John Leach, who was not interested in this instrument and was willing to part. OL 568; window 21 × 8.5; bore ø at foot 13.7 × 13.2 (wider east-west); all covered d + 50 cents, though very prone to fly to overblown; thumb + 3 fingers g♯-50 cents. On loan to the Bate Collection *(x 4079)*.

XII   158   *The Bamboo Sax; Maui Xaphoon,* Brian Lee Wittman, PO Box 1163, Paia, Hawaii 96779, USA; U.S. patent D262035. "Each xaphoon is individually made, by the inventor, of carefully selected wild bamboo from the rainforests of East Maui." A chalumeau, cylindrical bore, a single internode of quite thick bamboo, dark stained. LH: high uppermost fingerhole, thumb, 3 quite close fingerholes; RH: 1 fingerhole, then 2 close together, then lowest. All holes burned, all ø c. 6.3, each in a slightly sunken field abraded rather than knife-cut. Integral mouthpiece formed at a node with an ordinary commercial tenor saxophone reed held with a normal brassed ligature. Thick bamboo reed cap. Lowest note middle C. In original cardboard box with introduction and instruction sheet. OL (incl cap) 322, without cap 306; end ø internal 18.7; bore above terminal knife-cut flare ø 13.3 × 14. Given by Jeffrey Green, Abu Tor, Jerusalem, November 1997.

CLARINETS

XI   78   Meråker Klarinett, *marked:* S F (Snorre Fjelldal, according to a letter from the museum). Reed and lay marked V. One-piece body of softwood (?pine), lathe-turned, with a small integral bell. The proximal end is shaped as a mouthpiece. A normal B♭ reed scraped very flat is held with a copper wire ligature, set for the lower lip. A very high thumbhole ø 6 , which doubles as a speaker, + 8 fingerholes (left hand uppermost) LH: ø 6.4, 6.4, 6.4, 6.4 slightly offset; RH: ø 6.1, 6.1, 5.9, 6 slightly offset, all burned in. Lowest note b♭, a tone below middle C. With red velvet-lined mouthpiece cap of the same wood. Bought from the Ringve Museum, Trondheim, which is now making the instrument available again. OL 388; bore ø at top of bell 17.5, contracting to c. 17; window 16.2 long × 5 wide; fingerhole ø all 6; bell ø 46.6; length of flare c. 22.

The Meråker clarinet was a Norwegian folk instrument deriving from the normal clarinet in the late eighteenth or early nineteenth century. It was revived in the twentieth century by Harald Gillan and is now being made again. See Bjørn Aksdal and also cassette.

The flat reed scrape seems to work better on classical clarinets also than simply chopping some of the thick end off an E♭ reed so that it will fit the lay, which seems to be the normal practice today among early-music clarinetists. I should be very surprised if the modern machine-made scrape were to be identical to that used in the eighteenth, or even the early nineteenth centuries. Just as modern clarinetists are far more casual about reeds than oboists and bassoonists, happy to buy them ready-made and discard any duds, rather than making them themselves or at least buying hand-made ones from a specialist (all oboists and bassoonists do one or the other, whether they play standard or early instruments, most of them making their own reeds), so early-music clarinetists seem very casual about reeds for their instruments. A very flat scrape, without a central spine, not only gives a more woody sound, which may or may not be "authentic," but it also seems not to force the pitch up. With a cut-down modern E♭ reed, most late eighteenth- and early nineteenth-century clarinets are much sharper in pitch than the flutes and oboes of the same period and make, and this seems to be inherently improbable and strongly suggests that there is something wrong with our modern set-up. Perhaps the reed scrape is the answer.

VII   198   Red-Hot Fountain Pen, inscription burned in and gilt filled: KEITH PROWSE / & CO LTD / 159 NEW BOND STREET / LONDON W.1 / 725, post-1925, when they moved to that address *(NLI)*. Ebonite, keyless. A white bronze ferrule at the top and bottom of the one-piece cylindrical body; there is no barrel and the mouthpiece, which takes a cut-down Eb reed, fits directly into the top of the body. Th + 8 finger-holes, ø 6.8, th 6.8, 4.5, 6.7, 6.7 offset to L, 6.7, 4.5, 6.7, 6.7 offset to R. A modern chalumeau, the Red-Hot Fountain Pen was popular as a specialty instrument for jazzing, as it was called, in night clubs and dance bands in the 1920s and 1930s. Bought after a Sotheby's auction; it was part-lot with a saxophone and fortunately the purchaser was not interested in it and only wanted the saxophone. OL 259; mouthpiece L 43.5 (+10.2, ø 11.6); body L (−10.9 ø 15.9) 215; bore narrowing to 12.65, ø at foot 12.4, widening to 17.8 over a flare 2.5 long; external ø 20.5; all covered e′ + 50 cents; next note up f♯ exactly. On loan to the Bate Collection *(x 4014)*. Illustrated in my *Romantic & Modern*, pl. 46. [φ1250].

The term "white bronze" is used here, following Philip Bate's example, because of the difficulty of distinguishing between German silver, nickel silver, maillechort, and other alloys of similar constituents and different patent names; all are based on copper with the addition of nickel and other minerals.

III   224   Small clarinet, *Barnes & Mullins / London*. Barnes & Mullins were established before 1921 *(NLI)*. Wood. Th ø 7.4 + 6 fingerholes ø 8.4, 8.2, 8.5, 7.7, 10.1, 8.2, keyless, the thumbhole almost on the mid-point, 200 mm from the bell end and 130 from the top of the body (c. 190 from the tip of the chipped mouthpiece), far too low to function as a speaker. Soprano saxophone ebonite mouthpiece, the end cut in a demilune, suggesting that the end of the reed had a curve the reverse of the normal, or perhaps it was bitten off to this shape. Lowest note ab below middle C when played with a replacement mouthpiece; the range seems limited to an octave, only in the chalumeau range. Presumably a child's chalumeau. OL 391 with original mouthpiece, 395 with replacement; original mouthpiece 60.5 (−10.6); body L (+9.2) 330, ø 13.25 (no bell flare). [φ 1234/B/19-20].

III 224b Replacement mouthpiece and cap 63.5 (- indeterminate).

I 166 Schools clarinet, stamped above the thumbhole "Germany." Wood. Th ø 6.3 + 7 fingerholes ø 4.7, 5.6, 6, 6, 4.8, 5.4 + 4.9, 5.4 + 4.9 + 1 frontal key above the highest fingerhole, the 2 lowest holes double. The mouthpiece is bigger than that for an E♭. Lowest pitch middle C. Designed to take children from the recorder to the clarinet. A chalumeau with German recorder fingering, and thus of little interest or success in England even when the cost was low enough to be worth using for this purpose (this one cost £4). After a few years, the price went up to much the level of the cheapest proper clarinets, which rendered the instrument useless. The metal ligature has been removed and the reed is now tied on to resemble the baroque type; the thumb rest has also been removed. Edgar Hunt, when he obtained one of these, now in the Bate Collection (4017) where the maker is noted as Willy Hopf of Taunus and the wood as maple (both of which probably apply to my instrument also), wrote an article suggesting the use of this instrument both as a *chalumeau* and also as a mock-trumpet, the seventeenth-century English equivalent. Bought from Leslie Sheppard, a dealer mainly selling cheap instruments to schools *(LGL5)*. OL 351; mouthpiece 69.5 (+16.1); body L (−17.8) 282, ø 13.5; bell ø 50 external, flare c. 35 long [φ 1234/C/10-11; 120/7-13; b/w sl].

III 170 B♭ clarinet, W MILHOUSE / LONDON / 337 OXFORD STT, (at that address 1797–1822 *(NLI)*). Boxwood with ivory mounts, 5 brass keys: two long keys for the left little finger for e/b´ (open) and f♯/c♯´´ (closed); a♭/e♭´´ for the right little finger; a´/ e´´´ at the top in front for the left forefinger, and a speaker at the top at the back for the left thumb. See below for details on these keys and their development. Thumbhole ø 6.3; fingerhole ø 6.2, 6.2, 6 // 6.9, 6.5, 7, R little finger 7.0. The mouthpiece is a replacement by Jim Howarth with a full-length lay but a long stem. The early clarinet mouthpiece had a stem long enough to pass right through the barrel, but the window was much shorter and narrower than on the modern mouthpiece, and the lay was also short, extending less than a centimetre beyond the bottom of the window, as on that for VI 244 below. One-piece lower body; i.e., the joints from the top are: barrel, left-hand or upper-body joint; right-hand or lower-body joint (each with three fingerholes) combined with the foot joint (with the right little-finger hole and all three little-finger keys), and bell. 2 slight bell cracks. OL 666; barrel L 598; body L (+20.2) 541; mouthpiece 71.5 (+35.4 ø 15); barrel 55.9 (−20.5) i.e., long tenon is an exact fit; upper body (+20.2 ø 14.1) 193 (+19.5 ø 13.7) (the upper body of a clarinet has two tenons, one to go into the barrel, the other into the lower body, hence the two +, and the two diameters); lower body and foot (−20.2) 230 (+17.5 ø 19); bell (−18.2) 118.8, ø 53, external 80.4; conicity begins just below the a♭/e♭″ key. Bought in an antique shop in Reading while there to play a *Messiah*. Illustrated in my *Romantic & Modern*, pl. X. [φ 1234/A/4-5; 120/1-3; b/w sl].

This is the last instrument catalogued before the Sheffield Exhibition in 1967, in preparation for which I had to catalogue everything that I had, so as to be able to decide what to exhibit. Everything up to volume III, page 170 is catalogued in more or less random order, as I put a hand on it, or as it was standing or hanging round a room. From page 172 onwards things are, theoretically at least, in accession order, save for whatever may have been forgotten at any stage and catalogued when found.

For all the clarinets, OL is overall length including the mouthpiece; barrel L is the length without the mouthpiece; body L is the length without the barrel (but including the upper tenon as + as usual). All three are given wherever possible because many instruments, in this and other collections, are missing the mouthpiece or both the mouthpiece and the barrel, and the figures may be useful for comparison. For fingerhole diameters, // shows a separate joint.

Johann Christoph Denner is said to have invented the clarinet and improved the chalumeau "around the beginning of the century" (the only evidence for this is Doppelmayr's much-quoted statement of 1730 to that effect). The unique surviving Denner chalumeau in Munich, a boxwood instrument with two keys much the size and shape of a treble recorder but with a large, though narrow-bore, clarinet-like mouthpiece, is presumed to be his "improved" model and is usually regarded today as being a tenor instrument; the shorter instrument, also with two keys, attributed to the otherwise unknown Stuehnwal (doubt has recently been cast on this reading of the mark; see *NLI*), which is slightly smaller in size than the Red-Hot Fountain Pen, VII 198, is regarded as a descant; both are illustrated on pl. 34 of my *Baroque & Classical* and in a number of other sources (NB that the mouthpiece of the "Stuehnwal" is now said not to be original). We simply do not know whether Denner jumped straight from truly idioglottal instruments such as Mersenne shows, similar to the Cretan pipe (VIII 150) above, to instruments such as these, or whether he or earlier makers had devised an intervening wooden instrument with a heteroglot clarinet-like mouthpiece which Denner then improved further. C. R. Day described (*RME Catalogue*, no. 221 and plate IVA, where unfortunately no details are visible) the only mock-trumpet known to have survived into recent times (it was lost from the Berlin Museum during World War II). This corresponded closely with the instructions in Walsh's tutor for the instrument (see Thurston Dart, "The Mock Trumpet"), suggesting quite strongly that Denner's was the first wooden model and that all previous chalumeaux were made of cane, were without keys, and were idioglot, even if they were elegantly covered with red (C. R. Day) or gilded (Walsh) leather. The instruction (Walsh, quoted by Dart) to 'put the Trumpet in your Mouth as far as the Gilded Leather, and blow pretty strong' implies that the reed, like that of the upcut idioglottal instruments described above, must be pouched wholly in the mouth and, like theirs, was fairly stiff. The four known editions of Walsh's publication, between 1698 and 1708 (only the last survives) cover exactly the period of Denner's "improvement," leaving little space for any more elaborate intervening instrument. Interestingly, all the written references to a keyless wooden *chalumeau* come from the 1730s and 1750s, well after Denner's presumed date for the "improvement."

It is clear from the repertoire and its dates cited by Colin Lawson that the *chalumeau* and clarinet were contemporary and were used in different musics and styles in the first half of the eighteenth century, and perhaps well into the second half. The one was not considered ancestral to the other, in the way in which we tend to think of them today; they were two different instruments with different functions and different repertoires. The chalumeau was almost entirely used in the fundamental register (that known later, and still today, on the clarinet as the chalumeau register), whereas the clarinet, for the first half of the eighteenth century, was used almost exclusively in the overblown register, as its name ("little clarino" or little trumpet) suggests. Equally, the name "mock trumpet" suggests that that instrument may also have been used in the upper register and therefore distinct from the chalumeau. Cary Karp suggested, in conversation, that adjustment of the reed may have enabled the chalumeau to play in either upper or lower register.

As a result of this divergence in use, two basic differences between the two instruments were the shape and size of the mouthpiece and reed, and the position of the thumb key. The long mouthpiece and reed of the chalumeau favoured the lower register, and the smaller mouthpiece and reed of the clarinet favoured the upper register—it is noteworthy that all three modern chalumeaux catalogued above have reeds and mouthpieces of clarinet proportions. Because the cylindrical bore means that the first overblown note is a twelfth above the fundamental, the fingers alone cannot fill this range, and one or two keys are needed to assist them to do so, both for spacing and because the finger resting on the touchpiece of a key can help to hold the instrument, whereas one lifted from a fingerhole cannot. On the chalumeau the thumb key was principally an extension key, for it was seldom required to act as a speaker-key, and it was therefore placed almost opposite the front key. That same key, on the early clarinet, because it had to perform three functions, producing the written a′ and, with the front key, bɦ′, as well as acting as a speaker to force the pitch into the upper range, from c″ onwards, was moved up towards the mouthpiece where it could better carry out these functions. The earliest surviving clarinets have only these two keys.

Eric Hoeprich has convincingly suggested that the reason for adding the lowest key, for eɦ/bɦ′, to the clarinet was to be able to move the speaker key to this better position, and perhaps at the same time change to the later arrangement where the speaker produces g♯′, the front key a′, and both together bɦ′. The lowest note of the early clarinets, before the addition of this key, was the written f below middle C. On a clarinet built in C, all holes closed would indeed produce that f. On a D clarinet it would sound the g a tone higher, and so on with other sizes. Like the chalumeau, the clarinet has always been built in a variety of sizes, and thus in different keys. To avoid confusing the player, the fingering on each size is the same for the same written notes. The resulting sound depends on the size and pitch of the instrument but the notes are always referred to by their written names. And because some authors refer to clarinet keywork by the notes produced in the upper register, and some by those in the lower register, the only secure way to avoid confusion is to use both, as here.

Two further keys were added around the middle of the eighteenth century, first a short one for the right little-finger for a♭/e♭″, the equivalent of the oboe's E♭ and the flute's D♯ key, and then a long one for the left little-finger, to open a hole just above the bell for f♯/c♯″. By this time the third key, for low e/b′, had been moved from the back, where it had been controlled by whichever thumb was the lower, to the side for the upper little finger where this second long lever was also to be controlled, now always by the left little-finger.

It was the addition of these two long keys that made woodwind players in general decide definitively which hand should be above the other. It must have seemed impracticable to fit both the low keys for the thumb at the back, and it was certainly impracticable to duplicate them on each side like the E♭ keys of the early oboe, whereas it had been possible to provide a forked touch for the a♭/e♭″ key to make it accessible to either hand. Players therefore decided that all should follow the majority, and left hand above right became almost universal. A very few instruments have been made, even into modern times, for those who were obdurately determined to play the other way (something that is now generally available only to recorder players who, even with the modern plastic instrument, can turn the foot joint to suit either hand).

With these five keys, which remained the standard number for many years, the clarinet became capable of almost anything required by composers of the classical period. This number of keys, resulting in a much heavier and more complex instrument than either the oboe or the transverse flute, was one of the reasons for the slow adoption of the clarinet. It was a classic example of the vicious circle. If there were few players, it was not worth writing for the instrument; if little music were written for it, there was no point in buying the instrument and learning to cope with the extra keys and all the problems of an upper register a twelfth above the lower, instead of the usual octave.

The five-key clarinet was used in England certainly from the 1750s, perhaps even earlier—we do not know how many keys Mr. Charles had, the

Hungarian virtuoso who was the first named clarinetist here, nor how many there were on the instrument for which Handel wrote, which one suspects was probably Mr. Charles's, though the likelihood is two keys as on most of the surviving instruments from the early period—and the five-key clarinet remained in use into the 1820s. A long sixth key for the right forefinger, controlling a hole at the side of the top of the upper body, was often added as an upper shake key, as on VI 244, but this remained an added convenience, rather than an essential. The earliest known English clarinets with the shake key (on these a short key for the left forefinger) are those by George Miller which are shown in the Zoffany portrait of *The Sharp Family* in the National Portrait Gallery in London, and which are now on loan from a descendant of that family to the Bate Collection (*x 4008* and *4009*), whence measured drawings and a postcard are available. They date from about 1760, but their shake key may have been added some years later—it was not an original fitting. On the Continent a more common sixth key was the cross key for c♯'/g♯'' at the bottom of the upper-body joint, but both there and here the five-key instrument also remained in use and indeed still appeared in makers' catalogues for cheap band instruments into the twentieth century.

VI   244   B♭ clarinet, James Wood, *marked:* [royal arms] / JS WOOD / PATENT / NEW COMPTON STRT / 50 / SOHO / LONDON, which can be dated from that inscription to 1816–1821 *(NLI)*; the other joints have a *fleur-de-lys* above the name (*NLI* says Prince-of-Wales feathers were used on some stamps and perhaps this may be what this is). Boxwood with ivory mounts. Divided lower body (i.e. separate lower body and foot). 6 brass keys, five as above and the sixth the normal shake. Thumbhole ø 6.2; fingerholes 5.6, 5.9, 5.9, // 7.3, 7.2, 7.2 // 7.8. The short-stem mouthpiece is original and is stamped I.WOOD just off-centre below the short lay; does the off-centre stamp indicate an oblique hold (e.g., like a Stanesby flute? All Stanesby *traverse* have the stamp on the head joint some degrees off the embouchure line; Stephen Preston has shown that aligning all the stamps, while maintaining the usual position of the embouchure against the lip, turns the finger-holes to a comfortable position. Are there similar advantages to an oblique hold for the clarinet, or was Wood careless in stamping this mouthpiece?). The barrel has Wood's patent tuning slide, no. 3797 of 1814. The ivory bell ring is a replacement. The boxwood mouthpiece cap may be original. Despite the possibilities of dating from addresses, patent dates, and so on, the divided lower body and the late beginning of the bell flare suggests that this is an earlier model than the Milhouse, though the short-stem mouthpiece is a late indication. OL 663; barrel L 599; body L (+18.8) 542; mouthpiece 66.3 (+19 ø 14); barrel (−19.8) 53.7 (−18.8) tuning slide projects 13.5; upper body (+18.8 ø 14) 198 (+17.4 ø 13.4); lower body (−18.4) 102 (+16.9 ø 13.4); foot (−17.1) 131 (+21.1 ø 18); bell (−21.4) 115, ø 58.5, 80 external; conicity begins below the f♯/c♯‴ key. Bought from a music shop in Darlington while lecturing at a summer school at which they operated the repair shop; it had been left with them for repair many years before and had neither been collected nor paid for. [φ 1237/38-39].

VI   186   B♭ clarinet, [star] / *Herouard / frères*, in an oval, Paris & La Couture, active 1835–1878 *(NLI)*. Boxwood with ivory mounts, 13 brass keys: The open f/c‴ is end-mounted on a long rod fixed above the touch of the side b/f♯‴ with rollers to the a♭/e♭‴; the two long keys also have rollers; cross b♭/ f″, side b/f♯″, cross c♯‴/g♯″, cross e♭‴/b♭″, side f′/c‴, side g♯″/d♯‴, front a′/e‴, upper shake, and rear speaker; many pads are missing. Thumbhole ø 6.8, fingerhole ø 6, 6.3, 6.3 // 7.5, 7.5, 7.5. The ebonite mouthpiece is a replacement, marked PARAMOUNT / JACK / HEYWORTH / MADE IN ENGLAND / 4 star, and the ligature is slightly too small; the upper body is slightly warped, but the lower body is so badly warped that when stood up it "walks." OL 665; barrel L 598; body L (+20.7) 532.3; mouthpiece L 71.7 (+17 ø 15); barrel L (−17.7) 66.5 (−21.8) bore ø 14.65; upper body L (+20.7 ø 14.5) 180 (+16.5 ø 14.7) lower body L (−17.8) 237 (+20 ø 21.7 — 15 level with the axle of the e/b′ key); bell (−20.4) 112, ø 59, 62.5 external. On loan to the Bate Collection *(x 4025)*. Given by Philip Bate, who had acquired it from Reginald Morley-Pegge. [φ 1237/34-36].

VII   20   B♭ clarinet, anon, probably French. Rosewood and brass (or very low nickel white bronze). Thirteen keys and brille for right hand. Not the usual simple system but an earlier version of the 13-key clarinet, probably that of Iwan Müller. The upper body is the same as the normal simple system but while the lower body has the usual brille and attached b/f♯″, the cross b♭/f″ is on the opposite side to the usual position, which does not affect its fingering, and the a♭/e♭″ has its own cross axle instead of a long axle; the f/c″ key (which is missing) was end-mounted, again on its own cross axle. Mouthpiece and S-shaped frontal speaker are also missing. Barrel is solidly jammed on top of the upper body and I cannot shift it without peril. Speaker hole ø 3; thumbhole ø 6.2 (a deep slot has been cut for the speaker touch); fingerhole ø 6.5, 6.5, 7.2 // 7.3, 7.5, 8 (hole for f/c″ key 12.5). The bell ring is loose. Barrel L 570; body L–; barrel (−16.7) 60.7 (−?) bore ø 14.8; upper body (+?) 174 (+16.1 ø 14.8); lower body and foot (−16.3) 227 (+20.7 ø 22); bell (−21.1) 106, ø c. 53, 76.5 external; conicity begins just above f♯/c♯″. Source unknown. [φ 1245].

XII   140   B♭ clarinet, anon. Lower body and bell only. Simple system with patent f♯/c♯″ (see below). Wood painted very dark brown, and white bronze. Body and bell are reluctant to separate and, since the instrument is anonymous, no useful purpose would be served by forcing them. Fingerhole ø 7, 7.3, 8.2. OL 331; lower body bore ø 14.8 (−17) 227 (+?); bell (−?) 105.5, ø c. 53, 76.5 external. Found uncatalogued; source unknown.

I   36   B♭ clarinet, BESSON, LONDON. Besson was established in London by 1858, and continued until 1950 *(NLI)*. All three marks are very faint: a ribbon above a five-pointed star; only that on the lower body is readable. Rosewood and white bronze, black plastic mouthpiece. Simple system. Right-hand brille with the usual attached b/f♯″; patent f♯/c♯″; both side and cross e♭′/b♭″—this is my only Franco-Belgian simple system to have the side e♭′/b♭″, though it is present on the German simple system by Lípa (III 200 in C below)—frontal speaker with S-shaped lever. Thumbhole ø 7.1; fingerhole ø 6.7, 6.2, 6.1 // 6.7, 7.3, 8. The barrel is a replacement for one lost by a repairer who was asked to glue up a crack. OL 635; barrel L 570; body L (+22) 516; mouthpiece 67 (+17.2 ø 14.4); barrel (−17.8) 53.2 (−20); upper body (+22 ø 15) 188 (+15.7 ø 15.1); lower body (−15.7) 225 (+20.9 ø 22); bell (−21) 105, ø 56, external 76.5; the conicity beginning by the f♯/c♯‴ key. Source unknown [φ 1234/Q/4–6].

The simple system was established by Eugène Albert in Brussels in 1862 on the basis of developments by Charles Sax of the 13-key clarinet, which had initially been devised by Iwan Müller in about 1810. It was used in England from the time of its invention into the middle of the twentieth century. In the latter part of that period, from around the 1930s onwards, it was used mainly by bandsmen and by unfortunate school-children, to their later confusion when they moved to a Boehm system, as they had to if they were to continue playing at all seriously. Its characteristics are 13 keys with, usually only on the right-hand, lower body joint, a brille (a pair of rings, resembling a pair of spectacles, *brille* in French, hence the name), with attached to it a small b/f♯‴ key, so that the brille closes it, and on a shorter axle, parallel with that of the brille, the cross b♭/f‴ key. The simple system also normally, though not invariably, included the patent f♯/c♯‴, an open-standing key (unlike the long f♯/c♯‴ key) mounted on the same axle as, and controlled by, the f/c‴ key for right little finger. Its axle runs parallel with that for the a♭/e♭‴ key, which has an extension lug allowing the long e/b′ key to close the new f♯/c♯‴, as well as the e/b′. The left-hand, upper body joint is much simpler with (from the bottom) the cross c♯/g♯‴, cross e♭′/b♭‴, side f′/c‴, side g♯′/d♯‴, front a′/e‴, upper shake as on the classical boxwood instruments, and speaker. It was quite usual to curve the speaker round to one side, or more commonly to the front, by using an S-shaped lever or a rod axle from the touch for the thumb at the back, to avoid condensation or saliva getting into the speaker hole and damaging the pad as well as obstructing the hole. From the mid-eighteenth century onwards such liquids were kept out of the thumbhole by projecting a short tube into the bore from that hole; presumably it was thought best to move the speaker to avoid having two such holes close together, lest they should set up unwelcome perturbations in the air column. In performance, despite the theoretical presence of a key for every note, a number of chromatic notes have to be cross-fingered as on the earlier instruments. The absence of the Boehm system's cluster of small side keys on the right-hand side for the right forefinger and the absence of the group of larger touches lower down for the right little finger are the immediate clues for recognition.

IV   196   B♭ clarinet, Hawkes, London. Bell *marked:* xx / CENTURY / [eagle on a globe] / HAWKES & SON / MAKERS / DENMAN STREET / PICCADILLY CIRCUS / LONDON W // ♭ / 14706 above bell (the flat sign indicating that it is low-pitch, A = 439 Hz). This mark 1895–1930 *(NLI)*. Chromium-plated metal, now corroded, single wall, skeleton model. Simple system, right hand brille and patent f♯/c♯″. Thumbhole ø 7.6; fingerhole ø 7.5, 7.9, 7.9, // 7.9, 8.5, 9.4. Cork-lapped joints between the hands and between the barrel and the upper body; the bell appears to have been made separately but seems to be permanently fixed. Music-holder socket immediately above the bell. Ebonite mouthpiece chipped. Bought in the Portobello Road street market. OL 672; barrel L 595; body L 560; mouthpiece 70.7 (chipped) (+16.5); barrel (−17.5) 35.9 (+27.9 ø 14.5); upper body (−27.9) 222 (+17); lower body and bell (−17.1) 335, ø 64.4 external; conicity begins by a♭/e♭″ key. [φ 1234/ K/39-40; 1234/Q/30-32; b/w sl].

Called the skeleton model because the tone holes all project as little tubes the length of the thickness of the wood, thus resembling the bones of a skeleton; double wall models have also been made, the inner wall the diameter of the bore, as here, and the outer the diameter of the normal wooden model. The pitch of every note is governed by the length of the bore, and the length of the fingerhole through the wood is part of the bore for that note. If the body is of thin metal instead of thick wood, that length through the wood must be preserved if the tuning is to remain correct. Hence these little projecting tubes for each fingerhole. The same thing is necessary on the metal flute and other instruments, but it is less obtrusive there because the holes of the Boehm system flute are wider than those of the clarinet in proportion to their length, and those of the saxophone and ophicleide are wider still.

XI   54   B♭ clarinet, FIRST / CLASS / HAWKES & SON / LONDON / 10739. This mark 1889–1930 *(NLI)*. Simple system with better quality keys than most, with patent f♯/c♯″. Frontal speaker, the touch broken off at the axle. Thumbhole ø 6.7 (nick hand-carved for speaker touch); fingerhole ø 7.6, 7.6, 7.1 // 6.6, 7.3, 8. A crack through the upper shake hole has been pinned. With patent tuning slide mouthpiece inserted into the barrel. OL 648; barrel L 586 including tuning slide screw; body L (+17.5) 509.5; mouthpiece 43.8 (+25.9 ø 14.5); barrel (−26.5) 73.5 (−19.1); upper body (+17.5 ø 14.8) 177 (+15.9 ø 14.8); lower body (−16.3) 230 (+20 ø 21.7); bell (−20.1) 103.7, ø c. 54.5, 78.8 external; the conicity starting just above the f/c″ key. Bought from a dealer outside the Bath auction rooms because of the interest of the tuning slide.

IV   36   B♭ clarinet, Martin frères, Paris, *marked:* [bee] / MARTIN FRES / A PARIS / [monogram MF] / [five medals] / GRAND PRIX. This mark 1875–1927 *(NLI)*, and with five medals probably post 1889. Simple system with patent f♯/c♯″ and frontal speaker. Thumbhole ø 6.5; fingerhole ø 7, 7.2, 7.2 // 6.8, 7.6, 8 all very sharp-edged, showing that the instrument has been little used. Ebonite mouthpiece. High pitch. Cork lapping had been increased with thread, transparent adhesive tape, and paper; the last two have been removed and more thread added. OL 640; barrel L 569; body L (+19.5) 506.5; mouthpiece 71.9 (+16.9 ø 14.8); barrel (−17.7) 62.6 (−20.4); upper body (+19.5 ø 14.6) 173 (+15.6 ø 14.75); lower body (−16.5) 227 (+19.3 ø 21.7); bell (−20.2) 105, ø 51.5, 77 external; the conicity starting above the f♯/c♯″ key. Purchased. [φ1234/A/0-1].

IV   34   B♭ clarinet, BAUMGÄRTEL, MÜLHAUSEN (Vogtland, c. 1903 according to *NLI* which knows only this instrument). The bell, which is unmarked, is a paler wood than the very dark African blackwood or ebony body joints, but the white bronze mounts are the same throughout. German simple system, devised by Carl Baermann (the son of Weber's clarinetist) and based on Iwan Müller's system, rather than Albert's, and the precursor of the Oehler system, with right-hand brille, no patent f♯/c♯‴, rollers for both little fingers, rear speaker, the high g♯/d♯‴ key a short one for the left forefinger rather than the longer key for the middle finger, but otherwise little different from the Franco-Belgian. Thumbhole ø 5.7; fingerhole ø 6.4, 6.4, 6.4 // 6.6, 6.6, 6.6. Barrel and mouthpiece missing. Body L (+21.6) 538.5; upper body (+21.6 ø 14.5) 199 (+17.4 ø 14.5); lower body (−17.5—socket cracked) 231 (+21.7 ø 22); bell (−22) 108, ø 53.5, 78.3 external; conicity beginning just above e/b′ key. Purchased. [φ 1234/A/2-3].

XI 244 B♭ clarinet, Russia. [Λ in a ribbon wreath] / Ц.90P / N 5481-77r . The mouthpiece marked Λ / /Ц.0-75К. Presumably the clarinet cost 90 roubles and the mouthpiece, from the same maker, 75 kopecks. All black plastic, rather more like bakelite than ebonite, with integrally moulded thumb rest, no mounts. Chrome keys with rollers for both little fingers. The upper-body joint is Oehler system except that there is no link from the speaker to the top ring of the brille; it has the cluster of four side keys for the right forefinger (two trills, and side f′/ c‴ and e♭′/b♭″), and the brille vent on ring I, also closed by the a′/e‴ key, to flatten the a′, and the vent on ring II, which is also closed by the cross e♭′/b♭″ key, to improve the left-hand fork. The lower body has the Oehler extra a♭/e♭′ from the left little finger, but only the simple-system two-ring brille without a forked-F vent, though with the high e‴ correcting device, a key attached to the upper of the two rings (ring IV) which is also closed by the normal (right little-finger) touch of the a♭/e♭′ key, and the normal patent f♯/c♯′. Thus it is not full Oehler but considerably more than the normal German simple system. Thumbhole ø 6.1; fingerhole ø 8, 7.7, 8 // 7.2, 7.6, 8.7. OL 656; barrel L 584; body L (+22.5) 536.5; mouthpiece 71 (+18 ø 14.8); barrel (−18.3) 49.5 (−23.8); upper body (+22.5 ø 14.9) 200 (+15.4 ø 14.9); lower body (−15.7) 227

(+19.7 ø 20.5); bell (−20.3) 108.5, ø 51, 73 external; conicity begins immediately above the e/b′ key. Bought Gardiner Houlgate auction, Bath, 10/12/93, lot 135.

The Oehler system combines the Albert system with various continental improvements to it, such as the left-hand rings, but also with devices from the German simple system, such as the forked touch to the c♯′/g♯″ key which allows it to be controlled by the left little finger, as usual, or by the right forefinger. There is, in fact, more than one Oehler system (as indeed there is more than one Boehm system model also) and instruments exist with much greater complexities than those of the above instrument. It is normally played with a string-tied reed, rather than a metal ligature, and it is, of course, the standard instrument in Germany and over much of eastern Europe.

III   162   B♭ clarinet, MAYER MARIX / PARIS, 1867–1890. Boehm system (standard or plain Boehm as patented by Klosé and Buffet save that the thumbhole is covered by a plate rather than by a ring and thus could not be measured). Fingerhole ø 4.5, 6.5, 7.6 // 7.5, 7.4, 8.3. No separate barrel: mouthpiece, 2 body joints, and bell. A crack at the top of the lower-body joint has been pinned. OL 660; barrel L 589; mouthpiece 72 (+16.8 ø 15.3); upper body (−17.5) 253 (+17.2 ø 14.6); lower body (−17.2) 233 (+21.6 ø 22.5); bell (−21.7) 102, ø 53, 78.5 external; conicity beginning just below f♯/c♯″. Bought from Bill Lewington as an example of the Boehm system. Illustrated in my *Romantic & Modern*, pl. 11. [φ 1234/P/9-12; 120/2; b/w sl].

The Boehm system clarinet was devised in Paris in 1844 by the player Hyacinthe Klosé and the maker Auguste Buffet, who was Boehm's licensee in Paris for flutes and who first devised the needle-spring to replace Boehm's gold leaf-spring. The mechanism was based on that of the 1832 conical Boehm flute, and few, if any, of the acoustical principles of the Boehm system were ever applied to the clarinet; fingerhole diameters, for example, have none of the relationship to bore diameter that is the essence of Boehm's *Schema* for the 1847 cylinder flute. It is unjust to the memory of Klosé and Buffet that it is Boehm's name that is always attached to the instrument, rather than theirs (and also somewhat unfair to Boehm!). It is indeed an adaptation of Boehm's mechanism that is used, but it was Klosé and Buffet who did the adapting and it was certainly they who devised the system that made its use practicable.

V   28   B♭ clarinet, NOBLET / FRANCE / 1854. Standard or plain Boehm system. Thumbhole ø 7.3; fingerhole ø 5.5, 6.7, 7.8, 7.7, 7.1, 8.8. Single wall (skeleton model) of cheap plated metal. One-piece body and bell. Music holder socket between the hands. Mouthpiece and barrel missing. Bell badly dented. The Noblet family was originally one of the leading French makers from the 1750s onwards (see Tula Giannini), but the business was sold to Leblanc in 1904 *(NLI)*, and Noblet is now Leblanc's name for their cheaper range. Body (+24.2) 543; bore ø 14.8; bell ø 76 external; conicity begins around the f♯/c♯″ key. Given by Paul Riemann, Des Moines, who said that the metal instruments were made for high school children as cheap instruments. [φ 6260/8/30-32].

Paul Riemann and his father had an instrument shop on a farm on the outskirts of Des Moines when I was a visiting professor in 1970, with plenty of space for barns and sheds. When damaged instruments came in from the local schools that were uneconomic or impracticable to repair, they would toss them into one of the sheds. He was very generous in giving me many such instruments of types which I did not have and which, even if unplayable, would still represent a type or a model. I was introduced to him by the kindness of James W. Luke.

V   30   B♭ clarinet, WILLIAM / NUERNBERGER / AMERICAN ARTIST on the front; 22162 / GERMANY on the back. Not in *NLI*. Standard or plain Boehm system. Speaker hole ø 3.5; thumbhole ø 8.2; fingerhole ø 5.6, 7.3, 8.8, 8.8, 8.8, 10.2. Single wall (skeleton model) metal. One-piece body and bell. Perceptibly better quality than the Noblet. Mouthpiece missing. Speaker broken off at the axle; only the touch survives. Barrel L 598; body L (+23) 532; barrel (−17.1) 69.3 (−25.2); body (+23 ø 14.8) 531; bell ø 74.9 external; conicity begins at f♯/ c♯″ key. Given by Paul Riemann, Des Moines, 1970. [φ 6260 /8/33-35].

III   222 a/b   Pair of clarinets in A (a) and B♭ (b). (a) *marked:* SUPERIOR / CLASS / HAWKES & SON / DENMAN STREET / PICCADILLY

CIRCUS / LONDON. (1895–1930) (b) the same save that EX-CELSIOR replaces SUPERIOR. They were used as a pair. Both rosewood and white bronze. Simple system, right-hand brille only, patent f♯/c♯″, frontal speaker with S-shaped lever from the thumb. The key forgings are very similar but not identical between the two. (a) has had the top of the upper body turned down for some reason. Both have loose ferrules on the barrel; (b) has several loose pads.

a) Thumbhole ⌀ 7.5; fingerhole ⌀ 6.2, 6.8, 6.3 // 6.5, 7.5, 7.9. OL 678, barrel L 610, body L (+20.2) 550; mouthpiece 71.5 (+17.5 ⌀ 15.5); barrel (−17.9) 57.5 (−21); upper body (+20.2 ⌀ 14.8) 207 (+16.9 ⌀ 14.6); lower body (−17.2) 240 (+20.2 ⌀ 22); bell (−20.6) 105, ⌀ 56, 74 external; conicity begins by f/c″ key.

b) Thumbhole ⌀ 6.8; fingerhole ⌀ 6.8, 7, 7.2 // 7, 7.4, 8. OL 642; barrel L 572; body L (+20.7) 515.5; mouthpiece 72.5 (+17.2 ⌀ 15); barrel (−18.8) 57.8 (−20.7); upper body (+20.7 ⌀ 14.8) 183 (+17.5 ⌀ 15); lower body (−17.8) 226 (+20.8 ⌀ 21.5); bell (−20.9) 105, ⌀ 56, 71.5 external; conicity begins by f♯/c♯″ key. Purchased. [φ 1234/A/14 of both].

Partly because of its acoustical behaviour, and partly because it does not respond well to cross-fingering, the clarinet is difficult to play in remote keys and it is therefore made in many sizes. Since the eighteenth century the three standard-size instruments have been those in B♭, for music in flat keys, in A, for sharp keys, and in C for that key and for music in G and F. The necessity for so many instruments, and the resulting expense, may well have been another of the reasons for the slow adoption of the instrument into the orchestra, even though it was already common in the military band, where flat keys are the norm and therefore the B♭ alone might suffice. Sax's addition of a low E♭ key at the bottom, to extend the range by a further semitone and thus obviate the need for an A clarinet, has never really caught on, although it remains available in most makers' catalogues; most players prefer not to transpose A parts on to the B♭ unless they have to. However, to save expense, the C clarinet is now very rare, all players being willing to transpose from that key on to the B♭, save for those with discriminating ears who can appreciate the considerable tonal difference between the two sizes. Transpositions of a whole tone are always easier than those of a semitone; the latter involves adding an excessive number of accidentals to the key signature. Equally, the soprano clarinet was made in D and in Eb, for sharp and flat keys. The D was the favourite instrument for the earliest solo works in the mid-eighteenth century (e.g., by composers such as Molter), and this size is still often used as a soprano in the orchestra, but it was later replaced as a solo instrument by the A for the sake of its smoother tone quality and its less clarino-like (not to say squeaky) sound. The Eb, due to its standard use as soprano in military bands, is found much more often than the D today, and is often used in its place.

I   38   C clarinet, Doré, Paris; the back of the lower body marked FOREIGN; the bell marked DORÉ / 629. Presumed to be early twentieth-century, one of only two instruments known to *NLI*. Rosewood and white bronze. Simple system with a brille for each hand and patent f♯/c♯‴. The upper brille has a plate at the top of ring I which is closed also by the touch of the a′/e‴ key to prevent the a′ from being too sharp (this was present also on the Russian XI 244 above). The g♯/d♯‴ key crosses over the a′/e‴ key. Rear speaker. The thumbhole is bushed with a white bronze tube which projects into the bore less than the speaker tube. Thumbhole ø 6; fingerhole ø 6.8, 6.8, 6.5 // 6.5, 7.1, 7.1. As on some other continental clarinets here the cross bb/f′ is on the opposite side from the normal simple system. High pitch. OL 584; barrel L 516; body L (+18.2) 464; mouthpiece 69 (+16.6 ø 14.5); barrel (−16.9) 50.2 (−18.8); upper body (+18.2 ø 14.5) 169 (+16 ø 15); lower body (−16.1) 208 (+18.5 ø 19.3); bell (−19) 88, ø c. 51 internal, 71.5 external; conicity begins by the e/b′ key. Bought from Thomas Coyne. [φ 1234/Q/7-9].

III   200   C clarinet, J.LÍPA / NYMBURK. Presumed to be early twentieth-century, the only instrument known to *NLI*. German simple system, 15 keys and 4 rings. Rollers on both little fingers. Speaker on the left side of the front, brought round from the thumb by a rod axle. A brille for each hand, ring I with the vent to flatten the a′, cross and side eb/bb‴ (the cross mounted on the brille axle), forked touch c♯′/ g♯″, patent f♯/c♯″, extra touch for a♭/e♭″ for the left little finger as on the Oehler system, the lower body as the Russian XI 244 save that it lacks the high e‴ correcting device. There are as many variants of the German simple system as there are of the Franco-Belgian. Thumbhole ø 5.5; fingerhole ø 6, 6, 6 // 6.8, 6.5, 6.5. OL 578; barrel L 512; body L (+18.5) 454; mouthpiece 67 (+16.9 ø 14.3); barrel (−17) 56.4 (−20.9); upper body (+18.5 ø 13.5) 165 (+15.6 ø 13.5); lower body (−15.7) 203 (+18.3 ø 19); bell (−19.7) 88, ø 46.5, external 68; conicity begins just above e/b′ key. Bought in Prague during the Galpin Society's First Foreign Tour (for which see *GSJ* XXI). Galpin Society Edinburgh Exhibition (1968) no. 150. [φ 1256/1/36-37; 1256/4/ 12-13].

VII 146 E♭ soprano clarinet, KEY / LONDON / [unicorn head]. 1807–55 (*NLI*); I would guess later rather than earlier within that range. Stained boxwood with ivory mounts. Originally 12 silver-plated keys, now 13, some of them now damaged, with added brilles on pillars (that for the left hand subsequently removed and the holes neatly plugged). The usual 6 keys in blocks with rollers on the left-hand long keys, plus cross b♭/f″ and b/f♯″ in blocks, sharing a common axle, side b/f♯″ in a saddle (players were always divided as to which finger they preferred to use for certain notes, and thus chose between side or cross keys, sometimes, as here, desiring the option of choice in performance between both cross and side), cross e♭/b♭″ in blocks, side f′/c‴ and side g♯/d♯‴ in saddles (the f′/c‴ is missing and the g♯/d♯‴ is a brass replacement, but the saddles are clearly original). A rather crude brass cross c♯′/ g♯‴ has been added in pillars screwed into the wood. Thumbhole ø 4.9; fingerhole ø 6, (hole for f′/c‴key 4.9, brass bushed) 5.7, 6 // 6.3, 6.3, 6.5, 5.8. The bell is fairly straight-sided (earlyish pattern), the lower body is one-piece. The barrel is marked BOOSEY & CO and appears to be sun-faded ebonite with white bronze ferrules. The brass tuning slide is fixed in the upper body joint, passes right through the barrel, and ends immediately below the bottom of the window in the mouthpiece. The mouthpiece is brown wood, unmarked, cracked longitudinally, and made to take a metal ligature (missing). The upper bell ring and upper end of the bell are cracked. OL 475; barrel L 418; body L (+ tuning slide projects 48.9) (+13) 381; mouthpiece 56 (+13.5); barrel (−14.5) 37.2 (−14.2); upper body (+ tuning slide projects 48.9) (+13 ø 12.5) 135 (+12.8 ø 12.2); lower body & foot (−13.3) 163 (+13.7 ø 15); bell (−13.7) 83.5, ø c. 50, 63 external; conicity begins around f♯/c♯″ key. Dorothy Crump Memorial Gift (see the note to the Adolphe Sax alto saxophone, VII 150, below for this). [φ 1245].

I   40   E♭ soprano clarinet, BOOSEY & CO / MAKERS / LONDON / 14021. Rosewood and white bronze. Simple system, right-hand brille only, patent f♯/c♯″. Thumbhole ø 6.5; fingerhole ø 6.8, 7.2, 6.7 // 6.5, 7.4, 7.8. Barrel (cracked) with tuning slide. Plastic mouthpiece marked Boosey & Hawkes Ltd / LONDON / B & C 2. All sockets metal lined. Frontal speaker with rod axle from right-angle rear touch. The thumb hook has been fitted at some time to the upper body; it is now on the lower body as usual. Bell ring missing. Lower screw on ligature broken. The top of the upper body is cracked. OL 485; barrel L 425; body L (+15.1) 392; mouthpiece 60 (+13.6 ø 14); barrel (−13.8) 34.3 (−16.5); upper body (+15.1 ø 13) 138 (+12.4 ø 13); lower body (−13.2) 171 (+15.7 ø 19); bell (−15.5) 79, ø 46 internal, 60 external; conicity begins by f/c″ key. [φ 1234/Q/ 10-12; 120/7-13].

IDIOGLOT CONICAL SINGLE REEDS—422.212

XI   258b   Stepped shawm, made by JM of three segments of aluminium tubing for demonstration. The narrowest segment accepts a single reed made of a goose quill and an oboe reed staple. The segments, each of a different bore diameter, are stepped into each other and are held together with adhesive gaffer tape. It is similar in length to a single length of aluminium tubing which is the same bore as the narrowest of the segments (XI 258a in 422.211), and the pair was constructed to show the different effects of cylindrical and conical reed-driven bores irrespective of the type of reed. The conical example overblows to the octave with either reed, whereas the cylindrical overblows to a twelfth. OL 282, narrow bore L 88, ø 7.1; medium bore L 133, ø 11; wide bore L 61, ø 13.

X   282   *Sarune getep* (small sarune), Batak, Sumatra. Thumb + 4 fingerholes, all ø c. 4.9. Similar in shape to the larger *sarune*. The body is a hardwood, the bell a soft wood with integral bell plate; the coconut-shell pirouette is attached to the flange by a cord. All is extremely precariously held together, for each section is only barely inserted into the next and it seems unwise to force them together harder. OL c. 230, body L 163, bell 68.7. The downcut single reed of bamboo (L 72.5) inserts c. 8 of that length into the top. Bore top ø 6.5 tapering to 5.3, bottom of body 5.7, bell 11.5, bell plate 49. Bought from Tim Byard-Jones who kindly brought it back for me.

XI   34   *Sarune kesil* (small sarune), Samosir Island, Lake Toba, North Sumatra. All the same wood, similar to that of X 282, but with a non-integral bell plate, coconut-shell pirouette, thumb + 4 fingerholes, all ø c. 5.5. OL 227, body L 175, bell 57.5, downcut bamboo single reed 55.7. Bore ø top of body 6.6, tapering to 4.25, bottom of body 7, bell 10, bell plate 56.3. A new instrument, made by F. Nopil or Nopit. Bought by Tony Bingham on my behalf.

The use of a single reed on a conical bore instrument is rare, but these Sumatran shawms are by no means unique in that respect. Bálint Sárosi shows shawms made from gourd sections with single reeds of goose quill, and some forms of whithorn (shawms made of coiled bark) also have single reeds. A further common example is the organ reed pipe, though these strictly come under 412 above. What is interesting with the Sumatran instruments (and adds doubt to the wisdom of Hornbostel's and Sachs's choice of reed form as the determinant factor, since by doing so it separates them) is that they are used as a pair with the larger *sarune* which has a double reed. For that reason, both these instruments are listed also among the double-reed conical shawms, each with the *sarune* with which it is paired.

HETEROGLOT CONICAL SINGLE REEDS—SAXOPHONES

The patent date is 21 March 1846 in Paris (no. 3226). However, Georges Kastner's account (p. 235ff; the main purpose of the book was to act as a puff for Adolphe Sax) of the visit of the French musicians to Sax in Brussels in 1842, to persuade him to move to Paris, makes it clear that the saxophone was already in existence and that it was one of the main factors which impelled them. From the morphology of the instrument, as well as from Kastner's evidence that the bass saxophone was the earliest of the family, it is obvious that its origin was an *ophicléïde* with a bass clarinet type mouthpiece. Charles Sax (the father) is known to have made *ophicléïdes*, and Adolphe had recently devised a new and improved bass clarinet, and had patented an *ophicléïde* with a reed mouthpiece in Belgium in 1838, 21 June, no. 145 (see Malou Haine & Ignace de Keyser, pp. 188-89). A normal ophicleide which Wally Horwood fitted up in this way, and which he has presented to the Bate Collection (691) where it is displayed among the saxophones, works surprisingly well and has a distinctively saxophone sound, quite different from that of an ophicleide with a normal cupped mouthpiece.

Sax produced two complete families of the saxophone, from soprano to bass (with occasional extensions at both ends). One family was in alternating E♭ and B♭ for military use, and the other was in alternating F and C, designed for orchestral use. The latter family is seldom seen today, save for the tenor, which has proved popular in dance bands and similar combinations, where it can easily read cello and bassoon parts, and where it is known as the C melody. The C soprano, which could read oboe and other treble parts with equal facility, is surprisingly rare.

VII   150   Alto saxophone in E♭, Adolphe Sax, Paris, 1859. Brass. Nineteen keys to low B♮ only. *Marked:* 13 / N° 19804 / Saxophone alto en Mi♭ breveté / *Adolphe Sax à Paris* / *Fteur de la Mson Milre de l'Empereur* / [monogram AS intertwined].

The 13 is added, presumably a band's number. The date is ascertained from Haine & de Keyser *op.cit.* No duplicate keys, but every thing (except the low B♭) is there. Right hand: C and E♭ for the little finger; plates IV, V, and VI also close the hole above IV; 2 keys only for side of forefinger, B♭ and high E—the C is forked. Left hand: little finger controls B, C♯, and G♯, and the side of the forefinger the high E♭, D, and F; the plates close the hole above plate I. Music-holder socket on the right at the top of the body. Wooden mouthpiece, well bitten; ligature missing. The end of the crook is thread lapped. The top of the crook has been patched. OL c. 601; bore L c. 1035; bore ø top of crook 12, bottom 24.5; bell ø 139. Illustrated in my *Romantic & Modern*, pl. XII with IV 70— φ 120/3. Dorothy Crump Memorial Gift. It was on loan to the Bate Collection (*x 52*) from 1981 but I offered it as a gift *in memoriam* Anthony Baines the day after his death was announced early in February, 1997, and this was accepted 27/5/1997. [φ 1249].

This was by far the most important of the instruments in the Dorothy Crump Memorial Gift. Mrs. Crump ran an orchestra, rehearsing every Sunday afternoon, in a barn on the farm in South Croydon, where she lived, and for 60 years it never gave a concert. In her latter years when, through arthritis and cataracts, she became incapable of conducting it for a full rehearsal, I did so, playing horn, timpani, or percussion on the occasions when she wanted to have a turn. After her death, her daughter Heather gave me six instruments in her memory. The choice of this saxophone, coming from this source, as a memorial to Tony Baines is especially appropriate because he gained his first conducting experience, apart from the prisoner-of-war camp, in that same orchestra after the War.

VI   188   Alto saxophone in E♭, brass, A. Morhange, Paris; *NLI* 1890–1900, successor to Mayer Marix (cf Boehm system clarinet III 162). *Marked:* [5-pointed star] / [a winged lady blowing a straight trumpet held in her right hand, her left holding an olive wreath, standing on a globe] / TRIOMPH / A.MORHANGE / PARIS / [star]. To low B♮ only. Simple system without automatic octaves. Right hand keys as the Sax, left hand also save that plate III does not close the hole above

plate I. Rollers for each little finger. The end of the crook
is cork-lapped. A number of springs needs replacement.
Music-holder socket at the top of the body. With home-
made sling of string and a celluloid bead. Wooden mouthpiece replaced by Philip Bate, ligature marked
J. HIGHAM LTD / MAKERS. In a case with a good stock of
reeds. Wooden protector plug for the top of the body. OL
c. 550; bore L c. 990 including mouthpiece; bore ø top of
crook 11.2, bottom of crook 22.9; bell ø external 114.
Bought at a Puttick & Simpson's (now Phillips) auction
20/9/73, lot 59. [φ 1237/40-42].

XII   12   Alto saxophone in E♭, a good working instrument to B♭,
c. 1930. *marked:* [sunburst containing a monogram] / René
Guénot / PARIS–FRANCE / [star] / ESSAYÉ PAR / L.MEYER /
GARDE REPUBLICAINE. According to *NLI*, Guénot was a
trade name used by A Douchet, a Paris woodwind dealer,
ante 1933–*post* 1950. Frosted silver plated, the key plates
polished. The crook ends with a screw tuning device. Automatic octaves, patent high F, articulated G♯, duplicate G♯
trill, A♯/B trill, extra E♭. Right hand as the Sax plus G♯ trill
and F♯ trill; plate VI closes V also and the extra E♭ lever
which normally hold down plate V—this is why plate VI
also holds it down, to free the E♭ lever without opening
hole V. IV-VI also close the left hand A♯/B trill. The thumb
has 3 levers, B♭, C, and high E. Left hand as the Sax plus
low B♭ and patent high F. 2 black plastic mouthpieces,
spare reeds in patent IOA box. The music holder socket is
broken off the top of the body (?a dry joint), and is loose
in the case compartment. With a black cord sling. In original case. OL c. 680; bore L c. 1010; bore ø top of crook
11.5, bottom of crook 22; bell ø c. 120. Given 22/10/94 by
Miss S. M. Winter whose late brother had bought it new
in the 1930s.

IV   128   Soprano saxophone in B♭, in alto (curved) shape. *Marked:*
[lyre] / BUFFET / *Crampon & Cie* / À PARIS / [monogram BC]
/ *Evette & Schaeffer* / *Ance Mon Buffet Crampon & Cie* / *18 &*
20 Passage du Gd Cerf / *Paris* / *25036.* Silver plated. Auto-

matic octaves, articulated G♯, A♯/B trill. A hole in the centre of plate VI is controlled by the right little finger—?an
extra E♭. The side of the right forefinger has 2 keys only, B♭
and C; the left forefinger also has only 2—there is no room
for a third. Rollers for both little fingers. Ebonite mouthpiece; the end of the crook is corked. Socket for a music
holder on the front of the top of the body. Pitch is *diapason
normal* (A = 435 Hz). James MacGillivray suggested that it
had been modified for a player lacking the bottom joint of
the right little finger, but the extra levers (rather like a
crab's "dead man's fingers") cross plates IV, V, & VI and duplicate the action of the *left* little-finger keys. The bell has
been repaired at some time with a patch. The touch and
linkage for the top octave key is missing. OL 430; bore L c.
710; bore ø top of crook 19, bottom 16.5. After I bought it
in the Tottenham Court Road, it went to Philip Bate, like
various other instruments because his collection was sys-
tematic whereas mine was more random, in exchange for a
Siccama flute (IV 202) and a Gautrot oboe (IV 204), with
the promise that I am to have the first refusal to buy it back
if he, or the Bate Collection, ever decide to dispose of it. It
is now on loan from him to the Bate Collection *(x 50)*. Anthony Arnold had it for many years from Anthony Baines
after it arrived in the Bate Collection for repair to the octave keys and for alignment of some keys, but he seems
never to have done anything to it. I eventually managed to
get it back from him after much effort and reiterated re-
quests. [φ 1234/D/18, 19, 24; b/w sl with IV 70].

IV   70   C melody saxophone, Couesnon, Paris, post-1900.
marked: EXPOSITION / UNIVERSELLE / DE PARIS / 1900 /
HORS CONCOURS / MEMBRE DU JURY / COUESNON & CIE /
FOURNISSEURS / DES BEAUX-ARTS / DU CONSERVATOIRE
NATIONAL / ET DE L'ARMEE / 94 RUE D'ANGOULÊME /
PARIS / [a fasces emblem with MONOPOLE] / 47488 / [a
grenade with 26]. Silver plated. The tenor of the F and C
set. Low pitch (probably made as *diapason normal*), with

case. Automatic octaves, articulated G♯, A♯/B trill. Extra lever for right thumb beside the thumb hook as a duplicate lever for low C. Ebonite mouthpiece. The end of the crook is thread lapped. OL 695; bore L c. 1310; bore ø top of crook 12.5, bottom 25; bell ø c. 123. Bought from Hoade. On loan to the Bate Collection *(x 57)*. Illustrated in my *Romantic & Modern*, pl.XII with VII 150. [φ 1234/D/21-23; b/w slide with IV 128; colour transparency with VII 150: 120/3].

VI   222   Tenor saxophone in B♭, *Dupont / Artist Ideal / Milano (NLI:* dealers c. 1930). Cheaply silver-plated brass. Automatic octaves but otherwise simple system as the Morhange alto. Music-holder socket on the side of the top of the body. The touch is broken off plate IV and, more seriously, much of the action is bent out of alignment. The end of the crook is cork-lapped plus string. With a plastic mouthpiece with moulded mark KING T ligature marked FRANCE. OL c. 800; bore L c. 1500; bore ø top of crook 12.3, bottom of crook 27; bell ø c. 150. Bought from Tony Bingham for my son to use, but found to be beyond repair. [φ 1236/6-8].

III   38a/b   2 bass saxophone mouthpieces, used for demonstration. Only one can be found; the other may now be on something in the Bate collection and if so, being unmarked, must be considered as a gift to that collection. Bought Bill Lewington. OL 131; bore ø 18.2 but contracting slightly to fit over the crook. [φ 1234/J/33; b/w slide].

REED HOOTERS WITH UNDETERMINED REED—412.1?

III   112f   Two klaxons mounted on a wooden board, played by depressing a plunger, dating from the days, early in the twentieth century, when motor horns, especially those of taxis, were of this type. One is aluminium painted and its identification plate has been removed. The other is black painted, the handle moulded HAND / KLAXON and has a metal plate on the side of which only THE KLAXON CO LTD is legible. Bought as drummer's effects for pantomime or as a general sound effect. I have to admit that I have no idea how a klaxon produces its sound, nor do I intend to dismantle these to find out. Some research may be possible. Listening to the sound suggests that they may simply be stridulators, something scraping against a diaphragm, so perhaps they do not belong here. [φ 1234/E/40-41].

Reeds

There are so many single reeds in my drawers and in instrument cases, all ephemeral and all, save those for bagpipe drones which are already noted in the double reed fascicle, ordinary modern commercial reeds for clarinet and saxophone, that there seems little point in listing them.

Part III
Free Reeds

FREE REEDS—412.13

A problem, specific to this group, is that there are two sizes of free reed, as Picken pointed out in *The New Oxford History of Music*, pp. 185–87. The smaller is that which is used to generate the sound of the instruments described in this fascicle. The larger, too large to be set in vibration initially by the breath, is plucked by hand and is known as the trump, jews harp, or *guimbarde* (Hornbostel & Sachs 121.2). Both sizes will function only if *the lamella vibrates through a closely fitting slot* (Hornbostel & Sachs 412.13). The larger instruments are sometimes known as lamellophones, regarding the reed (or feather as British trump players sometimes call it) as a tongue or lamella, but this can cause confusion because the same term is use for the African *sansa*, *mbira*, or *kalimba* (Hornbostel & Sachs 122), instruments whose lamellæ are plucked by fingers or thumbs but which are arranged, like those of a musical box, in a comb pattern. Both the blown free reed and the trump may well have originated in South East Asia, where even the most cursory examination will reveal forms of each which are identical in pattern, distinguished only by their size and by the way in which they are played. More problematic is the New Guinea form of trump, a curved segment of bamboo, for which there is no direct parallel among the blown free reeds—the blown free reed is anyway unknown in Oceania. There also exist large struck lamellophones from New Guinea and a very large instrument from New Zealand, a tongue of a rotten tree (possibly deliberately carved), which is struck by a club; all are illustrated by Hans Fischer (original edition, p. 23 & figs. 26–28; English translation—it is essential to use the revised edition, not the first—p. 37 and figs. 26–28). It is possible, bearing in mind the standard theory that things begin large and that great size is gradually ameliorated into something more manageable and more portable, that these large, struck lamellæ are the initial forms of the trump and thus perhaps of the free reed—they do share the essential characteristic of *vibrating through a . . . slot*—but there is never likely to be any evidence either for or against such an hypothesis.

III   50a-c   Two large bamboo tubes with a brass free reed fitted, made for demonstration. They can be blown both through the reed and from the end of the tube, the latter method allowing others to see the reed vibrate. The reed in each case is cut idioglottally with a knife in a thin brass plate which is then attached to the bamboo over a hole cut in its wall. (a) had a pointed, triangular reed fixed with adhesive tape but cannot now (July 1997) be found (some duplicate instruments have been given to colleagues without the gift being noted in the register); (b) has a rectangular reed which was held to the bamboo with beeswax but which has now been remade with the brass plate attached by gaffer tape (a specially strong-backed adhesive tape). The reed has been slightly weakened at the root by scraping to make it easier to blow. Also (c) a small sheet of brass with a rectangular reed cut in it, the reed painted red to show the vibrating portion more clearly; the gap between the end of the reed and the sheet in which it is cut is slightly too wide for it to work properly. (b) OL 272; bore ø 26.3, wall thickness 3.6; reed L c. 19, W 3.4; pitch G♯ + 20 cents. (c) brass 124 × 43, th 0.5; reed L 28.5, W 3.9. [φ (a) 1234/L/3; (b) 1234/Z/26; (c) 3021/2/37].

IV 46 Free-reed horn, probably German. Cow horn with scalloped bell (19 rounded leaves) and screwed-on horn mouthpiece which covers a free reed. Perhaps a child's instrument, though such horns have been made for those incapable of blowing a proper horn; L. C. R. Cameron refers to English hunting horns provided with a similar reed, pointing out that these are useful for anybody in cold weather. Thus this may be an amateur's version of the German forester's horn II 232. A split ring through a hole in the horn near the bell holds a small ring; a similar hole near the mouthpiece must have held another to take the other end of a sling. The brass reed is in a shallot or frame of a zinc-like metal, similar to the original T-handles of the Kirchner-Pauken II 142, used when decent metal was difficult to get after World War I; therefore this horn may also be dated to the early 1920s. Bought Aladdin's Cave, Croydon. OL 300; L round convex curve c. 330; bell ø 72.3 × 67.5; reed W 2.5; pitch A-30 cents. [φ 1234/B/7].

In 422.3 *infra* are the Karen side-blown free-reed horns of horn and wood. A conventional acoustician, trained to accept that all free reed instruments produce only one pitch for each reed, would place them here, as required by Hornbostel & Sachs. However, because experiment has shown that the pitch produced is that of the air column of the horn, not that of the reed, these are listed under 422.3 and not here. Further experiment with some of the instruments that are here may show that they also should be there.

V   82   Free-reed conch, perhaps China. Small conch with a plastic mouthpiece containing two free reeds; the reeds are rectangular copper and inaccessible. They are set across the air stream in the Chinese manner, not along it as is usual in Europe, but both sound only on blow. Presumably a carnival instrument—it seems rather elaborate for a toy. Bought in a Chinese shop (the only evidence that it is Chinese) in Cleveland, Ohio. However, because the shell is *Busycon carica* Gmelia (knobbed whelk), which is east-coast North American, from Massachusetts to Georgia, the origin may be American. OL 186, conch L 155; max ø 82; pitches D♯ and F♯. [φ 6260/6/3-4].

X   188   Multiple instrument, plastic, MADE IN HONG KONG. A two-tongue ratchet, the tongues in blue plastic, the 8-star cogs in white; the green and white handle a duct whistle; the block at the other end with a white boss below containing a siren, and a white boss above containing two free reeds with rounded ends set across the airstream like those of the conch above, sounding only on blow.

X   182   Pitch pipe, free reed, tunable from f′ to f″ chromatic by moving a pointer on a scale, the other end of which moves a bridle on the reed. The reed looks to be brass. The tuning is very approximate: f′, f♯′, g′ + 5 cents, g♯′ + 7, a′ + 7 (= 442 Hz), b♭′ + 15, b♮′ + 17, c″ + 20 (= 529.3 Hz), c♯″ + 10, d″ + 30, e♭″ + 33, e″ + 25, f″ + 25, slide right in f♯″ − 35, but F♮ is the highest pitch marked. OL 69.5; tube L 48.5; ø 12.9; reed L inaccessible. See my *Scales of Music*.

XI   272   Reed pitchpipe. Sprite Chromatic Pitch Pipe / E / Japan / W. Range e′–e″ chromatic. White plastic disc with protruding single mouthpiece; the brown plastic central block with a brass reed in each channel, marked with each pitch name. As the central block turns, it presents the required channel to the mouthpiece; a window at the back allows the air to escape past the reed. The pitch names are also numbered, from 1 to 12, A being 1, with two E's, each numbered 8, but the lower coloured black like all the others, the higher coloured red. The tuning is reasonable: e′, f′, f♯′ + 5 cents, g′ + 5, g♯′ + 5, a′ 0 (440 Hz), b♭′ − 10, b♮′ − 5, c″ (523.3 Hz), c♯″ − 10, d″ + 5, e♭″ − 5, e″ + 5. Bought from Russell Acott, Oxford, for *set*7 Exhibition at the Bate Collection, mounted for the British Association for Science, March 1994 (see my *Scales of Music*). OL 86.2; ø 65.

XI 274 Reed pitchpipe. M.HÖHNER'S / *(Vocal, Full Chromatic)* / "TRUTONE" PITCH PIPE / N°P3 / *The World's Best!* / A–440 / MADE IN GERMANY · FABRIQUE EN ALLEMAGNE—a mouthorgan with a sliding mask (marked U.S.A. Pat. 1710502. D.R.P. 489790.) to open only one of twelve channels at a time. An arrow points to the note required, which are marked in staff notation, c′-c″ chromatic, and in English note names (C♯, not *Cis*, etc). A wooden bar has the brass reed plate on the note-name side only; the reeds are blow only. The channel mask and slider, and the resonance chamber on each side of the bar are chromium plated. This is badly out of tune at the bottom, the three lowest notes being very variable: c′ − 50 cents (a quartertone flat!); c♯′ − 25-30; d′ − 20; e♭′ − 5, e′ − 5, f′, f♯′, g′ − 3, g♯′, a′ − 5 (438.7 Hz), b♭′ − 5, b♮′?, c″ + 5 (524.8 Hz). It is sufficiently out of tune to be very little use, despite the claim on the box. In its original blue, pink-lined cardboard box, wrapped in a sheet of thin paper advertising other Höhner products and giving all main agent addresses. Bought from Russell Acott, Oxford, for *set*7 Exhibition as the preceding. OL 125; W 30, th of wood and plate 7, max th 18.2.

XI 276a-d Free reed pitchpipes:

  a) four-tube pitchpipe for violin, presumably German. Each tube marked on the back G D A E. A rectangular plate with one side a flat resonance chamber marked

VIOLINE / [lyre with a treble clef superimposed, surrounded by a wreath]; on the other side the four half
tube chambers. L 55.2; W 37; th 10; pitches a′ + 40
cents (450 Hz), e″ + 15, d′ + 30, g + 20.

b) six-tube guitar pitchpipe, box marked Pyramid Gitarre
Stimmpfeife A-440 Made in Germany; each tube la-
belled in French: low Mi indeterminate, La-20 cents
(435 Hz), Re-50, Sol + 5, Si + 10, Mi + 12. OL 58,
OW 41.5, ø each pipe 10. Probably bought from Chas.
Foote when I bought a guitar for my son.

c) a white bronze tube with a single free reed, one end
stamped A. OL 38; ø 10; pitch A at 456 Hz.

d) another similar marked C, a plated tube. OL 32.3; ø 9.5;
pitch C + 35 cents, 534 Hz or C at A = 449 Hz.

These may have been bought with a large batch of violin mutes from
Richard Beare, and not catalogued until preparing the *set*7 Exhibition.

IV   12e-f   e) A chromium plated violin mute with a single pitchpipe
on the top, thus fulfilling the dual functions of adding
weight and being a tuning aid. Sounds 434 Hz, only one
vibration from A at *diapason normal* (French pitch).
Bought Richard Beare. Tube L 32.3; ø 9.5; Ht tube to
bottom of mute 33.5. [φ 1234/Y/41-42].

f) another similar, white bronze, but the middle spur of the
mute is divided to act as a string gauge, widest for D,
next A, next G, narrowest for E, each marked with 3 dots
for different gauges on each string, in this order because
a covered G would have been used but a plain gut D and
A. The widest dot for D is 1.9 mm. Tube L 32.4; ø 8.7;
Ht 30.8; pitch A at 452 Hz, 2 Hz below the old high
pitch (Old Philharmonic). Presumably bought from
Richard Beare, but not catalogued until preparing the
*set*7 Exhibition.

Mouthorgans

The East and South-East Asian mouthorgans are all coupled systems of a
free reed and an air column. On the instruments of this type, while the

shape and design of the instrument varies widely from one area to another, the reeds are all within a common air chamber, but they are constructed so that each reed will sound only when an air column is coupled to it. This is achieved by fitting a group of pipes into the air chamber, each pipe either with a reed cut idioglottaly from it, or more commonly set heteroglottaly into it; the acoustic length of each pipe is normally regulated either by its length or by slots cut in the pipe towards one or each end. Thus the physical length need not be the length of the air column, and can be regulated for the sake of appearance. The slots are usually facing within the circle or raft of reeds where they are not immediately apparent to the eye and do not detract from the appearance. Coupling is achieved by closing a fingerhole, and each reed will sound only when the hole in its pipe is closed. In some areas, one or more pipes are closed with wax or a peg to provide a drone. On the Chinese and Japanese mouthorgans, one or two pipes are dummies, present, like the *façade* pipes on many church organs, solely to please the eye (though it may be arguable that they were once functional and, like the forked touch on the C-key of the oboe and the F-key on the bassoon, may have been retained, rather than abandoned, because they looked well). Most, probably all, such mouthorgans, certainly all those that I know, have reeds which work on both blow and draw, producing the same pitch in both directions. Thus the sound can be almost continuous. This, of course, is a basic difference from the European instruments, all of which, whether mouth or bellows blown, are designed to sound in only one direction.

The fact that the Asiatic mouthorgans are a coupled system of reed and pipe, unlike the European mouthorgans and reed organs, makes one wonder whether indeed they should be here or whether they should, like the Karen horns, be under 422.3. There is still much work to be done here.

The mouthorgan is endemic in South-East Asia. The existence in China is well-known and well-established over a period of three thousand or more years, and there are surviving instruments from the mid-fifth century B.C., from the tomb of the Marquis Yi (see von Falkenhausen) and perhaps others earlier; certainly there is earlier iconographic evidence. The migration thence to Japan in the eighth century A.D. or so (cf Kenzo Hayashi *et alii*) is also well-established. It would seem that the Korean instrument (see Chang Sa-Hun) also derives from the Chinese, presumably rather earlier than the Japanese since it is suggested that the Chinese instrument may have gone to Japan via Korea, but today it is used only in rituals of Chinese origin, although Keith Howard suggests that there may be some interest in reviving its use as a new sonority for Korean music among the younger composers.

All three of these mouthorgans are of the same type: originally a gourd, but now a wooden (in Korea), lacquer (in Japan), or metal (in China) bowl with a circle of pipes round the periphery of its flat top arranged, according to traditional sources, so that the tops of the pipes are in the shape of a phoenix's wings. The Marquis Yi pipe was of this pattern, as are those preserved in the Shôsôin, and as are those in all three of those countries to this day.

Similar mouthorgans of pipes standing in a gourd, but arranged in a less formal pattern, are used from Assam, in the north, through Burma in the west into Malaya and down at least as far as Borneo in the south, and also in Cambodia, Laos, and southern Vietnam in the east (as well as the specific sources for each of those countries, see Paul Collaer, *Südostasien*, pp. 27, 52–53, 67, 70, 128), and were known in Java where they can be seen on the walls of the ninth century (A.D.) temple of Borobudur (A. J. Bernet Kempers, fig. 200, also reproduced in Jaap Kunst, fig. 12). In some cases the pipes stand together, usually bound with sennet or similar material, whereas in others they are splayed. The eighth-century instrument from Sassanid Persia, which is discussed below, is a century or so earlier than the Borobudur mouthorgan. Its form, which is closer to the Chinese than to any of the South-East Asian or Indonesian patterns, suggests transmission through direct trade contact with China, e.g., for silk, rather than through indirect transmission.

A quite different type, morphologically, is found in the centre of the circle outlined above, in Thailand, and is also prevalent today in Laos. This consists of a double raft of pipes, two rafts side by side, each pipe in each raft the same physical length as its neighbour in the other raft, but tuned again with a slot cut in the bamboo both above and below the wind chamber, for the pipes project through the wooden windchamber, usually with more of the length above the chamber than below. The earliest appearance of this type so far noted is illustrated on Dongson Culture bronze drums from Hoàng Ha and Ngoc Lu in Tonkin (North Vietnam), dating from around the second century B.C. (see Kempers, *Kettledrums*).

A third type, with pipes more casually arranged, but again projecting below the wind chest as well as above, is known from Laos and, somewhat differently arranged, is seen here (X 22) from the Hmong people of Thailand.

It is more than time that someone prepared a coherent typology of the Asian mouthorgan. The information presently available makes it quite impossible to build any coherent distribution map of types, whether geographically or chronologically.

I   172   Mouthorgan, *sheng*, China. 17 bamboo pipes, one of them a dummy (the first anti-clockwise from the gap), standing in a circle round the top of a chromium-plated brass cup-shaped reed chamber. A gap in the circle allows the player to reach the fingerhole on the inner side of two pipes with the right forefinger. A metal reed pinned heteroglottally in a metal plate is set into the side of each pipe (except the dummy) near its base. A tuning slot is cut in each pipe by drilling two holes 25 mm apart and joining them with a knife cut on each side of the diameter of the hole; the slots are then partly filled with wax if necessary to fine-tune them. Thus the acoustic lengths differ from the physical lengths. A bamboo strip round the pipes holds them together. Each pipe, except the dummy, has a fingerhole bushed with brass scrim and, as noted above, will only sound when that fingerhole is closed. The third and fourth pipes, clockwise from the gap, have their hole on the inner side of the circle, to be closed by the right forefinger. Bowl H 72, ø c. 92, W c. 145; mouthpipe H 45.5, W 30, ø 14; pipes clockwise from the gap, all but one measured on draw: 1: G♯ ht 143 (the heights (ht) are from the surface of the bowl to the top of each pipe; they are not the sounding lengths of the resonators); 2: G − 30 cents ht 179; 3: F♯ − 15 ht 223; 4: G♯ − 10 ht 300; 5: C♯ ht 420; 6: C − 45 ht 300; 7: B ht 224; 8: E − 20 ht 181; 9: G − 20 ht 148; 10: high C♯ ht 148; 11: B − 15 ht 178; 12: G♯ − 40 on blow, silent on draw, ht 221; 13: D − 15 ht 300; 14: D − 20 ht 419; 15: A − 10 ht 298; 16: E − 15 ht 220; 17: silent ht 179. Bought from Collet's Chinese Bookshop, where it had been ordered, with other Chinese instruments, by Peter Crossley-Holland but not purchased because the delivery time had been so long that they were no longer required. These instruments are now available quite easily, but this was not so in the 1960s. [φ 1234/A/6-7; 2 b/w slides; illus. R&M pl. 26, 120/5].

A. C. Moule, while giving only 15 active pipes, lists which pipes make acceptable chords with which others; thus this instrument is the only one in Chinese music which is intended to produce harmony, or at least clusters of sounds, which may not be regarded as harmony in the European sense, rather than monophony or heterophony. Moule numbers the pipes clockwise from the gap: 1 a dummy; 2 *Fan*, G±, used with 10; 3 *Kung*, F♯, used with 7 and 11; 4 *Ch'î*, E, used with 15; 5 *I*, C, used alone; 6 *Fan*, G, used alone; 7 *Ssû*, B, used with 11 an octave higher; 8 *Chî*, E, used with 15; 10 *I*, used alone; 11 *Wu*, B, used with 7 and 8; 12 *Liu*, A, used with 14 and 15; 13 *Shang*, D, used with 6; 14 *Shang*, D, used with 13; 15 *Ho*, A, used with 3. Discrepancies, omissions, and anomalies will be noted. 8 and 4 are not identical; 5 and 10 share a name but are a semitone apart, and so on. Moule says that gentle blowing causes the pipes to cipher and that strong blowing produces the notes wanted. However, he says, that suction is the correct method. Eta Harich-Schneider, at a demonstration at the Horniman Museum on a Japanese *shō*, which is a similar instrument, deriving from the *sheng*, used both blowing and suction to achieve continuous sounds and controlled *crescendo* and *diminuendo*.

VIII   160   Mouthorgan, *sheng*, China. Reed chamber only. Very thin lacquered wood, which is the traditional material, though the origin was probably gourd; ivory face to blow pipe and pierced ivory or bone hole in the base. Blow-pipe very slightly offset to the right of vertical so that the pipes lean to the left when blown. Holes for 17 pipes. A wooden block inside the cup supported the pipes and was held in position with black wax, as is the mouthpipe; it looks as though there may be chambers under the wax to allow condensation to escape through the pierced base plate. Once a good quality instrument, before it lost its pipes, much better than I 172. Given by Tony Bingham. OH 60; ø 72.8; OW with mouthpipe 99; ø pipe holes 6.5; mouthpipe face Ht 38.3, W 20, square mouthhole 8.7 × 8.1.

VI 138 Mouthorgan, *angkuluri*, Iban People, Sarawak, Borneo. 7 pipes, one of which ciphers, two of them with wooden caps, one with a flaring wooden bell, held with wax (some missing) in a gourd wind chamber with a long curved integral mouthpipe. The pipes are held in a tight circle by two bands of sennet. Clockwise, starting with the shortest pipe, 1: with a wooden cap, and with the fingerhole just above the gourd; 2: the longest, with a wooden flared bell, the fingerhole just above the first sennet band; 3: second shortest, with a wooden cap, the fingerhole by the gourd; 4: second longest, fingerhole above sennet; 5: a little shorter, fingerhole by gourd; 6: only about 2 mm shorter than 4, fingerhole above sennet; 7: inaccessible in the centre of the circle—it is presumably this pipe which ciphers and which is intended as a drone. The gourd, caps and flared bell dark brown; the pipes stained reddish. Probably a tourist instrument; brought back and given by Zaire Novack who bought it from the Sarawak Arts Council, Kuching. OL 840; OW with mouthpipe c. 235; ø gourd c. 82; pitch: leaks too much to measure. [φ 14/5/10-12]

V 54a/b Two mouthorgans, *khāēn*, Thailand. 16 pipes in a double raft, 8 in each rank, with a wooden reed chamber part way down the raft. The reed chambers marked in white paint: PONETOOM. NAKAE on one side, and NAKORNPANOM. THAILAND on the other. The two rafts are parallel for the physical length of the pipes, but the acoustic length is fixed by slots cut in the inner face of each pipe, both above and below the reed chamber. Each pipe has a fingerhole burned in, the two longest (next to the mouth hole of the reed chamber) low down for the thumbs, and the two furthest (and shortest) lower than the others for the little fingers. The pipes are arranged, in each rank, 2 longest, the same length, and then six steps. All the pipes are slightly stained by heat in a mottled pattern. There are wooden spacer-bars between the two ranks, one above the reed chamber and one below. The pipes are held together by bands of twisted leaf near the bottom, near the top of the shortest pipe, and near the top of the longest. Each of the middle and the lower bands has a small loop twisted in it, which can be used to hang the instrument on a hook. The pipes are held into the reed chamber by black wax, now too dried out to prevent leaks. When the instruments were bought one (b) did not function, but it was purchased nevertheless (at a discount) to break its reed chamber free so that the bronze reeds may be seen.

a) OL 910 (the 4 longest pipes) 755 (next pair), 706, 660, 642, 626 (shortest pair); OW (reed chamber) 136; W (raft) 88; Th (reed chamber) c. 62, raft 32. The pipes leaked too much to measure the pitches.

b) there is a wooden spacer in the middle of the reed chamber, also, which has a general slot for all the pipes, not individual holes. The reeds face outwards, towards the walls of the chamber, and each fingerhole is on the same face as the reed. Each reed is a small sheet of very thin (little more than scrim) bronze, each with the reed cut from it idioglottally. The higher-pitched reeds are pointed, narrowly triangular, like that of the Philippine trump (V 198); the lower reeds are rectangular, some slightly tapering. A few have been tuned by scraping at the hinge. It is a reasonable assumption that this description applies also to (a). Some pipes have been removed so that they can be used for demonstration at lectures and later replaced, and at least one has been shortened to fit into a case, and therefore any of the three highest pairs may now be left/right reversed because there is no way to tell which way they were facing before they were removed. The pipes have now (August 1997) all been turned so that the reeds are facing inwards and the tuning slots outwards so that they may be seen and measured. Bought Cargo, a Chinese shop in Cleveland, Ohio. OL 880, 742, 685, 650, 639, 625, 450. The other dimensions were not taken since the instrument is no longer whole. Acoustic lengths from the longest, R and L for each pair, measured from the lower edge of the upper tuning slot to the upper edge of the lower slot (all approximate, and NB the *caveat* above, *re* possible reversal of the three highest pairs): 652 and 260; 545 and 505; 356 (recut—originally 465) and 492; 320 and 425; 270 and 386; 363 and 237; 206 and 197; 175 and 156. It would seem probable that the position of the fingerhole or vent is irrelevant to the pitch, since the position varies according to whether it is for thumb, long finger, or little finger, and this has therefore not been measured. [φ 6260/6/9-10].

See Laurence E. R. Picken *et alii, Khāēn* for details of manufacture, materials, and so forth. Picken shows that the reeds of these instruments, which are made from a specific coin, are the most carefully made of all mouthorgans, and has suggested that these instruments are a refined development of the Chinese, rather than a simpler precursor. I have not removed any of the reeds of (b) from their pipe to measure lengths and thicknesses.

Both the Chinese and the Thai mouthorgans have been known intermittently in Europe, or on its fringes, for a considerable period. The well-known eighth-century late-Sassanid silver vessel in the Musée des Beaux Arts, Lyons (Farmer, *Islam*, Abb. 8-9, and elsewhere) shows a Chinese mouthorgan as well as a *pipa*-style *'ud* (Abb. 8), a harp and a shawm (Abb. 7), and an hourglass drum and an indeterminate figure (Abb. 9). Mersenne (Proposition XXXV, p. 308) shows a Thai mouthorgan (upside down) with a detail drawing of the reed. Neither seems to have attracted general interest in their respective periods, good examples of instruments failing to be adopted until musical styles and social conditions were ready for them. It was the Chinese instruments which were eventually to be the origin of all European free-reed instruments. It is said that one of these arrived in St. Petersburg in the late eighteenth century and that its reeds were then copied for some organ stops in contrast with the normal organ reeds, such as V 214 above, which, until then, had all been beating reeds. According to Peter Williams (*A New History*) the earliest free-reed stops are in organs in the area which is now eastern Germany. Thereafter, the idea spread throughout Europe, with Grenié's reed organ and its successors, for which see below.

X   22a/b   Pair of mouthorgans, bass (a) and treble (b), *raj qeej*, Hmong People, Thailand. Each has 5 curved narrow bamboo pipes and one straight wide one which has a wooden plug attached to stop the fingerhole so that it can be used as a drone, and on (a) with 4 reeds and on (b) with 3. Used in pairs for funeral rites and ancestor cult. A gift because, after ordering them from photographs, I had waited so long for them to arrive, from Marten Timmer of Ganesha. The larger is one of the largest mouthorgans known, only exceeded, to my knowledge, by some of those of Further India.

b) has a long red-painted wooden body with long narrow mouthpipe and a wide medial swelling where the pipes are set, split laterally and presumably hollowed out, held together with 8 aluminium bands; there were at least 10 bands originally because the end of the mouthpipe, where one must have been placed, is broken off, and there are the marks where another one is missing from the distal end of the body. The bands were fixed before the body was painted. The six pipes pass vertically through the body, each through its own hole. The two left-hand narrow pipes have ferrous metal bands round the lower end; two of the right-hand pipes had such bands, now missing; the shortest pipe has its lower end broken off and presumably also had such a band. The pipes now fit loosely in their holes and can be moved up to show the reeds, cut idioglottally in thin brass(?) sheet, with parallel sides but the free end diagonally pointed, unlike the reeds of other pipes which are either triangular or rectangular with a square-cut end. The wide pipe has three reeds. Each pipe has a fingerhole. The wooden plug for the wide pipe is attached to the mouthpipe with string. There are no tuning vents. The first pipe on the right is the wide pipe, L c. 385, ø 29; the next is L 570, ø 14, the third L c. 620, ø 12.5. The first lefthand pipe is broken at the bottom, ø 12.5, the second L c. 780, ø 13, the third L 690, ø 14.7. The body L is now c. 515 and the maximum width is 86 and height 61. The pipes are angled through the body so that the lower ends are splayed and the upper tied together. Judging from paint marks and reeds, all the pipes projected about 130 below the body, and various heights according to their lengths above.

a) the larger, is unpainted and still retains some wax to hold the six pipes in position. The body now has 4 aluminium bands, though there are marks suggesting that there were several more, and two red cloth bands at the distal end. The wide pipe has four reeds and again there is a wooden plug to stop its hole. Each pipe has had the bark removed from the lower end, each of which projects about 155 below the body. Each pipe is closed by a node about 80 above the lower end, save for the widest whose node was pierced with a hot iron to make a small hole; this and the removal of the bark applies to (b) also. The pipe lengths are in the same order. Right-hand: widest L 645, ø 49, second c. 930, ø 18, third c. 1020, ø 19.5; left-hand c. 85, ø 18.5, second 1290, ø 19, and third 1150 ø 19 but since all are curved they are difficult to measure more than approximately. All the diameters of both instruments are external. Body L 765, max width 81.5, height 57.

VIII 230   Mouthorgan, *khāēn*, Thailand. A miniature instrument with only 6 short pipes made as a souvenir for tourists. No fingerholes so that all the reeds sound all the time, but each has two tuning slots. Useful, however, for demonstration of the general shape and type, since it is small enough to be packed easily. OL 425. Bought Global Village Crafts, South Pemberton.

V 248   Six pipes of a mouthorgan, with some feather decoration, probably Sarawak, with a central bracing stick, the gourd or other wind-chamber missing. However, it is possible that these come from the Naga of Assam, in which case they are only half the set; because I thought that I had pipes from two mouthorgans and gave one group (the smaller) to Josef Marx, only thinking later that this might be a Naga mouthorgan, which have their pipes in two groups in one gourd. Bamboo reeds, idio-weighted, one with additional tuning wax, identical in pattern to the reeds of the flat bamboo trumps of that area. Each pipe has a neatly cut triangular fingerhole. The reeds (one is missing) are set into the pipes with wax, close to the bottom ends which are closed by a node. Three pipes, including the longest pipe are cut off diagonally at the top, OL 890, 560, 555; three are cut off flat, all three 562. All are held together by a sennet band, and the longest has held to it by a band the root of something made of bamboo which might have been a reedcap. All these details, and comparison with a mouthorgan in the Pitt Rivers Museum, suggest that Sarawak is the most likely source, in which case the two sets were indeed from two instruments! Bought Fairclough. [φ 6260/2/4-6; detail of the reed 14/7/22-23].

III   52 a   Miniature mouthorgan, *harmonica*, Höhner / Made in / Germany. 8 reeds (4 blow + 4 draw) arranged as usual in four pairs, each with two chambers, one above the other, 1 diatonic octave, c″-c‴. Not just a toy or something to hang on a watch-chain, though useful in both respects, but used by music-hall artists who can conceal it within the mouth cavity and still produce simple melodies. OL 35 mm; width 13. [φ1241; col sl]

The European mouthorgan was invented either in Germany or by Charles Wheatstone in England (there were, and remain, a number of conflicting claims to the invention). According to *Grove* (*sv* harmonica), Buschmann invented a tuning device, perhaps similar to some of those above, which could be played melodically, as, with some effort, those above could be played also, while Wheatstone, soon afterwards, produced his symphonium, which was designed for playing music, as a compact instrument for social use. Other German workers took Buschmann's model and turned it into the instrument we know today. While widely popular in light and informal music-making, it was only with Larry Adler that the harmonica became regarded as in any way a serious instrument for which composers might write. Instruments vary considerably in complexity from the simplest diatonic to the fully chromatic, and in shape from the familiar horizontal model to end-blown models with a series of keys laid out like a piano keyboard, these being mainly for children.

III   52b   Mouthorgan, *harmonica*, Hero / Harmonica / Made in China; on the box: Shanghai. Forty-eight reeds (24 blow + 24 draw).

Wooden body with brass plate on each side and chromium-plated resonance chamber on each side. Pitches: lowest g, then c chord on blow, d chord on draw, and so on OL 178, OW 29.5, maximum th 24.5. The normal European mouthorgan, cheaply manufactured in China for export. [φ 1234/Z/ 15-16; illus. *Romantic & Modern* pl. 26, 120/5-10].

VIII 132 Mouthorgan, *harmonica*, anon. Body of a small, cheap instrument with the resonance chambers removed from each side to show the reeds when demonstrating. Twenty-eight reeds (14 blow + 14 draw). Lowest note is b, then d, then a g chord. The usual wooden body with a brass plate on each side. OL 118, OW 27, maximum th 11. Given by my son Simon.

XII 168 Small green plastic instrument, found in the garden, presumably tossed over from next door. Similar to those sold by the Early Learning Centre in Oxford, and probably from that source. Faintly stamped SUPER / MIDGE-MONICA /#/ MADE IN ENGLAND. Eight single chambers; the whiteish plastic reeds and their shallots appear to be idioglottal, each morticed into the green plastic body, and the pitches are purely random. OL 76, OW 25, maximum th 15.5.

VI 56 Mouthorgan, MADE IN FRANCE, brass, probably early twentieth century, though an identical instrument is shown in Thibouville Lamy's 1956 catalogue as a toy cornet. In folded trumpet shape with 8 pistons, with the touchpieces at the bottom, each containing a free reed, which sounds when the piston is depressed. Blown as a trumpet (which is possible), the instrument produces a g´ which is not affected by depressing pistons. When blown as a mouthorgan, the pistons produce one diatonic octave c´-c´´, sufficiently well in tune that resultants may be heard when chords are played—the reeds are independent so that chords are possible. A good quality child's toy in brass; similar toys, in the shape of almost any wind instrument, are now made of plastic. OL 270, OH 65, bell ø 70. Bought Phillips & Harris. [φ14/8/38; illustrated my *Romantic & Modern* pl. 26, 120/5].

Reed Organs

The reed organ was invented in France by Gabriel-Joseph Grenié around 1810, and the harmonium by Alexandre François Debain in 1840. The American organ, which sucks the air past the reeds, instead of blowing it like the harmonium, was invented only a few years later by Jacob Alexandre, also in Paris; it derives its name from its greater popularity as a system in America. It seems to have been a much more stable system. Reed organs of both sorts became immensely popular; they were cheap enough for domestic use (cheaper than a piano, since reeds were cheaper than strings and there was no need to use good quality wood for a soundboard, nor to make the instrument strong enough to withstand string tension, nor was there need for the cost of regular tuning, since free reeds will stand in tune for many years), and far cheaper than a pipe organ, but could cover the same range, from a 32-foot C to the highest treble pitch audible. Since a reed organ need be no larger than an upright piano (and many, such as VI 46 below, were far smaller), these factors of size and cost made it the ideal instrument for the chapels of those non-established cults which did not, until much later, gain moneyed and middle-class support. It was also useful, as Berlioz points out, as a substitute for the pipe organ in the theatre and the smaller opera house.

VI   46   Folding Harmonium, England, late-nineteenth century. There is no maker's name but the serial number 1714 is stamped on the reed block; there are some other inked and pencilled numbers. 3 octaves c-c″. Bone naturals with ebony sharps. There are two ranks of reeds, four stops (the left-hand knob missing as is that for the swell lever), and a swell lever which lifts the lid of the reed compartment. The pedals for the bellows are covered with carpet, as is common on such instruments. The front board, which would hide the pedals and side pieces when it is folded into its box, is missing, as is the music desk (there is a hole for it in each cheek), and the brass handles on each side of the box for carrying do not appear to be original. Instrument width 575 mm; height opened fully up 745; *stichmass* (NB only two octaves) f-f′ 293. Some work was done for me a long time ago by James Howarth on the bellows, but more is now needed.

The two supports fold in half to collapse the instrument and the trunking for the air runs up through these from the bellows. The repeated folding damages this trunking and causes air leaks. A wooden cross-bar fits into a bracket on each of these supports and holds them rigid when the instrument is erected. The two left-hand stops produce two different sounds, but the two right-hand knobs have no perceptible effect. Bought in a junk shop in Consort Road, Peckham, where I was told that it had been used by a local street busker who played to cinema and music hall queues in South London; the marks where his carrying straps were fixed to the case are still visible. Very similar instruments were made by R. F. Stevens of Kentish Town (Ord-Hume, pl. 21-23 and others) well into the twentieth century. Such instruments were widely used for revival meetings and for street-corner services, being easily portable. Kipling refers to such use in his story *The Village that Voted the Earth was Flat*. [φ 6260/9/28-31; illus. *Romantic & Modern* pl. 26 & 27, 120/5].

III	166 a	Set of american-organ reeds, all the Cs from 16-foot to 1½ inches. (the 8-foot is a C♯). Stuck on a piece of hardboard to show the different sizes. Bought from H. J. Fletcher Newman. [φ 1284/1, 5, 8, 9].
III	166 b	A French harmonium reed for the 32-foot CC, lead-loaded, marked UT and a five-pointed star on the front, 14 on the back. OL 92, OW 14. Bought from H. J. Fletcher Newman. [φ col sl].
III	166 c-	Small American-organ reeds for experiment (trying to reconstruct a free-reed pipe with fingerholes) and demonstration. a′, c″, e″, a″, c‴, e‴, a‴, c⁗, e⁗, c⁗′. Also some larger ones, 2 empty frames for CC♯, and an FF♯ to try (unsuccessfully) to make a trump. Bought from H. J. Fletcher Newman. Also two bamboo pipes, each with a hole burned near the closed end, surrounded by beeswax in which I tried to fix one of these smaller reeds to produce a pipe with free reed and fingerholes, each with 6 fingerholes burned in. One 453 long, the other 280. Neither worked.

Also a brown paper envelope of reeds, some fragmentary, from an unknown concertina, given by Philip Bate. They fit the slots on the concertina reed-tester IV 198 and three have therefore been left *in situ* there, two in the test slots and one on the plaque.

IV   152   Set of 3 octaves of steel reeds in brass frames in their original paper wrapper for harmonium, France. Bought from James Howarth. [φ 1234/P/34].

IV   124a   Knee-organ, *flautina* or *harmoni-flute*, Busson / Breveté SGDG / Paris, nineteenth century. Three octave f-f˝ keyboard, *stichmass* 412. One rocker and 2 stop buttons above the keyboard, 1 button below. The box opens like a drawer from the frame. The bellows leak too much to ascertain what each stop does. Three ivories are missing, from the middle C, and the G and B above. It can be played either resting on the knees, one hand controlling the bellows, the other the keyboard, or fitted to a stand (not present) with a pedal to operate the bellows. This type of instrument seems to be intermediary between the harmonium and the accordion. However, the concertina is indubitably earlier, and which led to which, with a plethora of inventors each producing their own form of small portable reed organ, is difficult, and probably impossible, to determine. Bought from Webster. [φ 1234/R/34-37; b/w slide].

IV   124b   A second, rather dilapidated example, which had been bought in Camden Passage by Philip Bate and passed on to me, was given to Arnold Myers in exchange for 3 pseudo-mediæval fiddle bows (IX 14). [φ 1234/R/38-41].

II   204   Concertina, Metzler & Co / Manufacturers / 35, 37, and 38 Gt. Marlborough Street / London / W. This address is not listed in *NLI*, but is presumably post-1842, when Metzler first moved to Great Marlborough Street (at no. 37), and perhaps pre-1881 when they moved to no. 42. The left hand side is numbered 57178, the handle stamped STEEL REEDS. Anglo-German system (different notes on press and draw from each button); 20 bone buttons. Lowest note c. Steel reeds are harsher, though louder, than brass. In original hexagonal mahogany box, which has lost its key (as well as its leather handle) and has therefore at some time been held closed with adhesive tape, which has marked it. Length of sides 90 mm; depth closed 160. Galpin Society Edinburgh exhibition 448. [φ 1256/2/21-24; b/w slide; illustrated my *Romantic & Modern* pl. IX and back of wrapper, colour 120/2].

IV 198 Concertina reed tester, Louis Lachenal, London, mid-nineteenth century. Outside of the original cardboard box marked: Louis Lachenal's / Newly Improved / Tuning Apparatus. Inside the lid: Louis Lachenal / Manufacturer of the newly improved / Full Compass, 48 keyed, Double Action / English Patent Concertinas / Prices from £2.2s to £8.8s. Space for two reeds, one the standard the other the one being tested. Heavily sprung so that the bellows can be pushed closed and then open under spring control (i.e., a standard pressure). Flap valve of chamois leather on the base so that air is drawn in past the reed as the bellows open. A thin brass plate is fitted by the reed beds to act as a plaque on which to scrape the reed to tune it. A sliding catch locks the tester closed. Hexagonal mahogany boards top and bottom 85 long, and three ball feet. Three reeds from III 166c (above) now fitted to show how it works. Given by Jack Haynes, Devizes. [φ 1234/K/4-6; details 14/4 38-40]

II 214 Accordion, faintly stamped by one end of the keyboard BUSSON / BREVETE / PARIS. Mid-nineteenth century. Sixteen keys for the right hand with mother-of-pearl plates and 2 thumb-levers. The keys alternate long and short; they are not laid out as the piano keyboard. The plate for the second short key is missing, as are the levers and stoppers for the two highest long keys. Several keys are linked, so that they open more than one stopper—whether this is intentional I do not know, but if so the melodic range is severely restricted. 2 thumb-levers and exhaust key for the left hand. Nicely decorated paper for the bellows. Inlaid marquetry on wooden body. Some reeds do not work; others cipher; 2 pads are missing. OL 305, OW 123, th 78 (bellows closed) + keyboard and bass thumb-lever box, c. 160 from keyboard thumb-levers to bass box. [φ 1234/K/42-3; illus. *Romantic & Modern* pl. IX and back of wrapper, colour 120/2].

I   48   Piano accordion, Mastertone, Foreign, c. 1920. Two octaves c-c‴, 12 basses. A fairly cheap instrument, not to be compared with V 226, but adequate, in its day, for the amateur. The plate covering the reeds on the keyboard side is missing. White plastic keys, grey/green pearl black keys and surround. Each key controls two holes, one for each direction; built-in vibrato. One high reed ciphers. OH 330, W 205 + keyboard, OW 340 Bought Aladdin's Cave, Croydon. [φ1234/R/15-17; b/w slide].

V   224   Piano accordion, Höhner Mignon, Germany. Two octaves c-c‴, 12 basses. Very small instrument, probably made for children. White and black plastic keys, green pearl body, metal grill over a cloth over the keyboard reeds. OH 275, W 150 + keyboard, OW c. 220. Bought in Thornton Heath. [φ 6260/9/16].

V   226   Piano accordion, Geraldo / Made in Germany, c. 1930. 2½ octaves G-E, 96 basses. Unlike the two previous, a serious instrument for the professional musician. The piano accordion is the most compact of all keyboard instruments. 2½ octaves is sufficient for most melodic use, and 96 basses are enough to provide all the harmonic support necessary for any dance and similar music (Geraldo was a famous danceband leader in London). Even the two previous instruments will cover most social music occasions. Not found January 1998. Bought at a West Central Synagogue bazaar, with case and tutor. [φ 6260/9/21]

REED-PIPES WITH FREE REEDS—422.3

I have experimented with making a free reed on a pipe with fingerholes (see III 166c above), but have not yet succeeded in producing one that will function; this is an instrument type still missing from this collection, and it is a serious lack.

VIII 226a/b Two free-reed horns, Karen people, Burma, (a) of black horn
and (b) of brown horn. The bell of each is approximately triangular in section, suggesting that both are of mythan horn.
Each has a long, pointed, triangular brass reed, set into the
concave side of the horn with black wax. Each has a fingerhole in the tip. Pitches, (a) c″, hole open c♯″; (b) a′+30 cents,
hole open c. b′. L down the side of the curve: (a) c. 325, (b) c.
370; bell ø (a) 77 × 52, (b) 80 × 59; reed L c. 21 on each, fingerhole ø 10.5 on each, bored to meet the natural cavity.
Bought from Global Village Crafts, South Pemberton.

In South-East Asia, mainly among the Karen, but also in the
Bangkok area on an instrument specifically associated with funerals, and
then sometimes made of ivory (the only ivory horns so far discovered which
are not African), a free reed, identical to that of a mouthorgan, is used on
side-blown horns instead of the player's lips. Experiment (blowing as a
trumpet through the fingerhole in the tip of the horn, while covering the
reed with the hand so that it cannot sound or leak, produces the same pitch
as blowing through the reed as a free-reed horn, with the fingerhole closed)
has shown that the pitch produced is that of the horn; i.e., the reed, in contrast with what the acousticians say, resonates the air cavity of the horn. Just
as with similarly designed, but lip-blown, instruments in Africa, opening
the fingerhole produces a second pitch (again in contrast with acousticians'
cant, which is that a free reed can produce only one pitch). Like all Asian
mouthorgans, these horns will sound on inspiration as well as aspiration.

It is because the pitch produced is that of the horn that these are
listed here and not under 412.13, which is where a conventional acoustician
would place them. One should experiment with some of the instruments
that are now in 412.13 to check whether they should be there or here.

X 48 Wooden free-reed horn, Burma. With a fingerhole in the tip.
Made, like a cornett, by splitting, gouging and reuniting a single piece of wood, the seam sealed with black wax. The reed
is now missing as are all seven of the bands which joined the
two pieces of wood (discolouration of the wood shows where
they were fitted) so that the instrument is now in two separate
halves. Interesting at least to be able to show the form. OL
445, bell ø 49.5 × 44, fingerhole ø c. 9, reed bed 32 × 8.
Bought from Tony Bingham in a bagful of shawms.

Part IV
Ribbon Reeds & Retreating Reeds

RIBBON REEDS, BARK REEDS, ETC—412.14

A ribbon reed is a strip of flexible material fixed in a close-fitting frame, held securely at each end and under some tension. The form familiar to children is the strip of grass tensioned between the two thumbs. A ribbon reed is, like a drum skin or a string, necessarily under some tension; as air passes across it, the reed produces a squeak, the pitch of the squeak varying probably according to the speed of the air and, less certainly, to variation in the tension of the ribbon, perhaps also to narrowing the gap between the ribbon and the frame. Some ribbons are more flexible than others (e.g., V 138a below is a rubber band whereas III 114a is a strip of cork); nevertheless both are capable of a wide range. Certainly it appears that it is the vibration of the ribbon itself which produces the sound, not the air passing across it, which would suggest that there is thus an analogy with the æolian harp, and the free reeds. In this respect the ribbon and free reeds differ from the double and single reeds which, by rapidly opening and closing, admit pulses of air to an air-column. With the ribbon and free reeds, there seem to be no such air pulses. However, both need a frame, the ribbon reed apparently less close-fitting than that of either the free reed or the trump, and it may be that the oscillation of the free reed to and fro in its frame (although, unlike the double and single reeds, there is no periodic opening and closure; air could still pass between reed and frame) suffices to produce such pulses also. It may then be that the oscillation of the ribbon reed also has this result, although, due to the fact that it is a ribbon, not a string, the reed must necessarily vibrate from side to side, towards one side of the frame and then towards the other, leaving, one would think, ample room for air to pass. As Hornbostel & Sachs point out, "The acoustics of this process has [sic] not yet been studied." Picken (*LERP* 365-66) states that the ribbon twists when blown, acting as an aerofoil, and then reverses its twist, and that it is this oscillation which creates the sound.

Whether the bark reeds and plastic equivalents should be included here is not certain. The bark reed is held in the mouth and flexed by the tongue or lips to tension it; the pitch produced appears to be controlled by the tension induced by this flexure, perhaps also by the speed of the airstream, and there appears to be an analogy with the flexatone and the musical saw. Unfortunately, I have not succeeded in producing a sound from these instruments, though Friedrich Schlütter tried to teach me when he gave me one (see IX 82); he played a plastic credit card, also.

Much more flexible than the bark, or even the leaves which are sometimes used, are the instruments such as V 150, but they appear to be of the same group. On the other hand, the Romanian carp scales are much thicker and more rigid (as are credit cards) and I am not certain whether they also belong here. Certainly, however, Alexandru (pp. 23–25) discusses together the leaf, the grass blade, the piece of birch bark, and the carp scale, and regards all four as musically equivalent, though he names them *"pseudoinstrumente."*

So far as I know, neither the ribbon reed nor the bark reed has yet been properly studied, other than by Picken's brief remark. The ribbon reed seems to be used only as an animal lure and as a toy; the bark reed and carp scale are virtuoso folk instruments, as Tiberiu Alexandru's recordings have shown. There does not seem, on these recordings, to be a link between pitch and volume, which is why the speed of the airstream was discounted as a factor above, but this may be illusory.

Cf remarks about the carp scale and similar instruments under 411, which is the other possible location for them.

III	114a	Bird of Prey and Owl Call, Acme, Birmingham. A strip of cork in a plastic holder. The dark brown plastic (?bakelite) is *bombé* shape with a cylindrical knob at each end. A gold transfer strip is lettered: BIRD OF PREY & OWL CALL. A narrow slit, 2.0 wide on the proximal side, into which to blow, wider, 6.0, at the back. Cork strip c. 0.5 thick, c. 10 wide. Tension of the strip cannot be varied—only the wind speed (which may alter the strip's tension). OL 71, free L of strip 48, ø terminal knobs 14.5 [φ 1234/G/22]
V	222	Ribbon reed, India. A slip of pale blue plastic, now broken, between two slightly curved pieces of bamboo, secured by a ligature of gold paper at either end. A child's toy. OL 61, W 6. Given by Laurence Picken, who bought it in The Cambridge Toyshop, after I gave him a Fox Call (V 138a). His is CUMAE 77.553. [φ 4528/1-2]
V	138a	Fox Call, Burnham Bros., Marble Falls, Texas. Close range model. A rubber band between two pieces of mottled brown plastic; the band subsequently perished and has been replaced, courtesy of H. M. Royal Mail; the bands which they use to bundle letters are exactly the right size. In its

original box with a descriptive leaflet of how successful the Burnham family are at catching coyotes, racoons, and foxes with such calls. Also an instruction leaflet and price list of other calls and instruction recordings. OL 88, OW 15, th 9, centre of gap 3 (the same on both sides, unlike III 114a). Bought Harry's Sport Shop, Grinnell, Iowa. Two were bought and one was given to Laurence Picken, now CUMAE 77.695. [φ 6260/7/33-34]

IX   82   Shield-shaped piece of birch bark, Friedrich Schlütter, Zella-Mehlis, East Germany. It seems to function as a beating reed against the upper lip as a block, but cf V 150 *infra*. The pitch depends on both finger tension against the bark and on mouth cavity shape. Schlütter demonstrated its use, but I have been unable to make it work, which inhibits investigation. W 43 × 35, th 0.5. Given by the maker during the joint ICTM and CIMCIM conference at Bratislava and Dolná Krupá (the Bratislava Composers' House).

V   150a/b   The Wonderful Double Throat or Swiss Warbler Bird Call, Registered Trade Mark "Swiss Warbler Bird Call" / MOTOHASHI TOY MFG CO / No 14251 No. 50644 / MADE IN JAPAN. A slip of polythene or similar plastic or perhaps goldbeater's skin is held on a semicircular piece of imitation leather by a metal band stamped JAPAN PAT. The label (above) is printed on the paper envelope which contains each. Also printed on the envelope are the instructions below. Six of them. Played like pieces of bark or carp scales between the lips: "The Only Original Bird Call and Prairie Whistle. Directions: For Use—Soak in water until thoroughly saturated then place on your tongue with the reed nearest your teeth and finished side of leather upwards and hiss gently at first, keep increasing the hiss for a louder sound in giving imitation of Birds and Beasts, you make variations with the tongue and lips. Any person following these directions we will guarantee they can imitate any Bird or Animal in a few minutes." A packet of four (a) were bought in a shop in Oscaloosa, Iowa, for 15 cents and four more (b) in a pink and transparent plastic box were bought from a slot machine in a gentlemen's lavatory at a Howard Johnson restaurant on the Pennsylvania Turnpike (eastbound) for 25 cents. Two of (a) were given to Laurence Picken (now CUMAE 77.694); hence the next entry. Those in the box have been left undisturbed in their envelopes. W(ø) 31 × 19; membrane c. 25 × 5 or 25 × 6.5 (two of (a) were measured). [φ 4528/3 and 14/7/29].

V   150 c   A similar instrument, *düdük*, Turkey, of stretched cellophane on a rhomboidal cardboard body, with a V-shaped cut-out for the membrane, clamped again with a semicircular metal strip. Wrapped in yellow cellophane and undisturbed. OW 22 × 14 × 14; V 4 × 3. Bought by Laurence Picken on the Anafartalar Caddesi, Ankara, from a pedlar who produced canary-like roulades on his own example (Picken's is listed as a canary whistle, CUMAE 77.241). Picken also obtained similar whistles from a street pedlar in Istanbul. Given in exchange for two of V 150a. See *LERP*, p. 367. [φ 4528/3 and 14/7/32].

Picken (*LERP* p. 365 ff) classes these instruments, and leaf whistles, as ribbon reeds, a decision which I have followed here.

XI   202   Two similar labial whistles, a membrane, perhaps of goldbeater's skin, clamped with a metal strip to a fibre semicircle, the latter stamped ETERNA / [bird] VOGELJAKOB. W(ø)28 × 18, membrane W(ø) 10 × 5. Bought by my wife at the Bruma Park market, Johannesburg, from a middle-aged white man who was whistling with one to show that they worked; he had it tucked up on to the palate behind the upper teeth.

RETREATING OR DILATING REEDS—412.15

Presumably Henry Balfour's retreating reed belongs here under 412 also. Balfour used this term on his labels in the Pitt Rivers Museum; I do not know whether he used it in printed publications. This is a grass stem, rice stalk, or similar object, with longitudinal slits. The player blows into the stem at one end and the slits dilate and contract under the pressure of the air stream, producing the sound as the air passes out of the instrument through the slits, in contrast with most other instruments, where the air passes into the instrument as it makes the sound. Balfour gave it that name because the walls of the stem move outwards (retreating from their position of rest) whereas other beating reeds close when they are blown. The instrument does not appear at all in the Hornbostel & Sachs *Systematik*, nor, of course, does the concept of a retreating reed. For this reason I have added a new number, 412.15, to include them. Picken cites some examples (with other references: *LERP* 347 ff), under the name of slit reeds, but he regards them as concussive reeds, which surely cannot be correct. The characteristic of concussive and percussive reeds is that they close in order to vibrate, whereas the retreating, dilating, or slit reed opens. It is also arguable, as suggested in the first section of the present catalogue, that the "brass" instruments should come under this head because this, as Campbell and Greated point out (p. 306 ff), is precisely what happens with the lips; they open outwards into the mouthpiece (I would thank Dr. Michael Leask for reminding me of this reference). Campbell and Greated use the term "outward-striking," in contrast with "inward-striking" which they use for double and single reeds; I prefer Balfour's term, or my own "dilating reeds," since these are more comprehensive and can include instruments other than those of Western art music, and also because free reeds, for example, cannot easily be called inward-striking.

I do not possess an example of grass; Balfour's in the Pitt Rivers are all immersed in a preservative liquid and therefore cannot be tried. However, my grandson, Eliezer Treuherz, seems to have discovered one modern example (XII 100 *infra*). While Balfour's retreating reed, and my grandson's instrument, belong under 412 because even though the grass stem "contains the vibrating air" there is no practical possibility of adding fingerholes, Ernst Emsheimer, however, recorded an instrument, the Lapp *fadno*, which combines a reed of this nature with fingerholes, and this would seem to require a new number in 422. Although at present there is no 422.4, it is tempting to leave that blank in case any example of the combination of a ribbon reed with a "wind instrument proper" should appear, and assign 422.5 to the *fadno*, thus retaining a numerical link between the 412 and 422 types of instrument. The player's lips, however, are sufficiently different from these retreating reeds that they still belong under 423.

XII   100   Eliphone. My grandson Eliezer Treuherz discovered at the age of two-and-a-half that the plastic binder strips which are triangular in section with one long side open, would produce sounds in two ways: when hummed into they function as a kazoo, and when blown into they function, it would seem, as retreating reeds, the open side dilating and springing closed under the pressure of the air. By delicately squeezing the strip with the hand, different pitches can be obtained. OL 333, W of back 8.2, W of sides 13.6. A note on the instrument has been published in *GSJ* XLI. A type specimen has been presented to the Bate Collection and is numbered 522. NB that it does need to be an unused binder strip; those that have been used for a while tend to be too open to function.

BIBLIOGRAPHY

Acht, Rob van, Jan Bouterse, and Piet Dhont, *Dutch Double Reed Instruments of the 17th and 18th Centuries, Collection Haags Gemeentemuseum*, Laaber-Verlag, Laaber, 1997.

Adkins, Cecil, "William Milhouse and the English Classical Oboe," *JAMIS* XXII, 1996.

Ahuir Cardells, Xavier, *Mètode de Dolçaina*, Generalitat Valènciana, 1989.

Aksdal, Bjørn, *Meråker Klarinetten*, Ringve Museum Skrifter No. 5, Trondheim, 1992.

Alexandru, Tiberiu, *Instrumentele Muzicale ale Poporului Romin*, Stat Pentru Literatură și Artă, București, 1956.

———, *Anthology of Rumanian Folk Music*, Electrocord, Bucharest, 6 10-inch 33 rpm discs, EPD 78, 81, 86, and 1015–1017, nd.

Ames, David and Anthony King, *Glossary of Hausa Music and its Social Contexts*, Northwestern University Press, Evanston, 1971.

Aubert, Laurent, *Les musiciens dans la société Newar*, Kathmandu, Musée d'ethnographie, Genève, 1988.

Baines, Anthony, *Bagpipes*, Pitt Rivers Museum, Oxford, 1960.

———, *Woodwind Instruments and their History*, Faber, 1957 *et seq*, which must be acknowledged as the source for many of the descriptions of keywork in this Catalogue.

Bate, Philip, *The Oboe*, Benn, 1956 *et seq*.

Becker, Heinz, *Zur Entwicklungsgeschichte der antiken und mittelalterlichen Rohrblattinstrumente*, Sikorski, Hamburg, 1966.

Berlioz, Hector, *Traité d'Instrumentation et d'Orchestration*, Paris, 1844.

Boydell, Barra, *The Crumborn and Other Renaissance Windcap Instruments*, Frits Knuf, Buren, 1982.

Cameron, L. C. R., The Hunting Horn, Köhler & Son, c. 1905; reprint Swaine, Adeney, Brigg & Sons, 1950.

Campbell, Murray and Clive Greated, *The Musician's Guide to Acoustics*, J. M. Dent & Sons, 1987.

Charoenchitt, Pratuan (ed), *Folk Music and Traditional Performing Arts of Thailand*, National Culture Commission Ministry of Education, Thailand, nd.

Christlieb, Don, *Pictorial Fingerings for Bassoon*, author, Los Angeles, 1971.

Collaer, Paul, *Südostasien—Musikgeschichte in Bildern* I:3, Deutsche Verlag für Musik, Leipzig, 1979.

Daniélou, Alain, *La Musique du Cambodge et du Laos*, Institut Français d'Indologie, Pondichéry, 1957.

Dart, R. Thurston, "The Mock Trumpet," *GSJ* VI, 1953.

Davison, M. H. Armstrong, "A Note on the History of the Northumbrian Small Pipes," *GSJ* XXII, 1969.

Day, C. R., *A Descriptive Catalogue of the Musical Instruments recently exhibited at the Royal Military Exhibition, London, 1890*, Eyre & Spottiswoode, 1891.

Dick, Alastair, "The Earlier History of the Shawm in India," *GSJ* XXXVII, 1984.

Emsheimer, Ernst, "A Lapp Musical Instrument," *Studia ethnomusicologica eurasiatica—Musikistoriska Museets Skrifter 1*, Musikhistoriska Museet, Stockholm, 1964 (originally in *Ethnos* 12:1/2, 1947).

Escalas i Llimona, Romà, *Museu de la Música 1 / Catàleg d'instruments*, Ayuntament de Barcelona, Barcelona, 1991.

Falkenhausen, Lothar von, *Suspended Music*, University of California Press, Berkeley, 1993.

Farmer, Henry George, *Islam—Musikgeschichte in Bildern* III:2, Deutsche Verlag für Musik, Leipzig, 1966.

Fischer, Hans, *Schallgeräte in Ozeanien*, Heitz, Strasbourg, 1958.

——, *Sound-Producing Instruments in Oceania*, Institute of Papua New Guinea Studies, revised edition, Boroko, 1986.

Fleischhauer, Günter, *Etrurien und Rom—Musikgeschichte in Bildern*, II:5, Deutsche Verlag für Musik, Leipzig, 1964.

Galpin, Francis W, *Old English Instruments of Music*, Methuen, 1910 *et seq*
———, "The Whistles and Reed Instruments of the American Indians of the N.W. Coast," *Proceedings of the Musical Association*, XXIX, 1902–3.

Galpin Society, *European Musical Instruments*, Edinburgh, 1968.

Giannini, Tula, *Great Flute Makers of France*, Tony Bingham, 1993.

Haine, Malou and Ignace de Keyser, *Catalogue des Instruments Sax au Musée Instrumental de Bruxelles*, Brussels, 1980.

Halfpenny, Eric, "The English 2- and 3-Keyed Hautboy," *GSJ* II, 1949.

Hayashi, Kenzo *et alii*, *Musical Instruments in the Shôsôin*, Nihon Keizai Shimbun Sha, Tokyo, 1967.

Haynes, Bruce, "Lully and the Rise of the Oboe as Ween in Works of Art," *Early Music* XVI:3, 1988.

Helffer, Mireille, *Mchod-rol*, CNRS, Paris, 1994.

Hickmann, Hans, *Ägypten, Musikgeschichte in Bildern*, II:1, Deutsche Verlag für Musik, Leipzig, 1961.

———, *Catalogue Général des Antiquités Égyptiennes du Musée du Caire, nos. 69201-69852—Instruments de Musique*, Cairo, 1949.

Hoeprich, Eric, "A Three-key Clarinet by J. C. Denner," *GSJ* XXXIV, 1981.

Hornbostel, Eric Moritz von and Curt Sachs, "Systematik der Musikinstrumente. Ein Versuch," *Zeitschrift für Ethnologie*, 1914, 4 and 5, English translation by Anthony C. Baines and Klaus P. Wachsmann, *GSJ* XIV, 1961.

Hunt, Edgar, "Some Light on the Chalumeau," *GSJ* XIV, 1961.

Howard, Keith, *Korean Musical Instruments*, Se-Kwang, Seoul, 1988.

Izikowitz, Karl Gustav, *Musical and other Sound Instruments of the South American Indians*, Elanders, Göteborg, 1934,

Jairazbhoy, Nazir, *A Musical Journey Through India*, UCLA, 1988.

———, *The Rāgs of North Indian Music*, Faber, 1971.

Jenkins, Jean and Poul Rovsing Olsen *Music and Musical Instruments in the World of Islam*, Horniman Museum, 1976

Kastner, Georges, *Manuel Général de Musique Militaire à l'Usage des Armées Françaises*, Didiot frères, Paris, 1848.

Kempers, A. J. Bernet, *Ageless Borobodur*, Servire, Wassenaar, 1976.

———, *The Kettledrums of Southeast Asia*, Balkema, Rotterdam, 1988.

Kipling, Rudyard, "The Village that Voted the Earth was Flat," 1913; collected in *A Diversity of Creatures*, Macmillan, 1917.

Kunst, Jaap, *Music in Java*, Martinus Nijhoff, The Hague, 1973.

Langwill, Lyndesay G., *An Index of Musical Wind Instrument Makers*, Author, Edinburgh, 5th ed. 1977. [see also Waterhouse]

Lawson, Colin, *The Chalumeau in Eighteenth-Century Music*, UMI Research Press, Ann Arbor, 1981.

L'Helgouach, Jean, *Ecole de Bombarde*, B.A.S., Quimper, 1956.

Marx, Josef, "The Tone of the Baroque Oboe," *GSJ* IV, 1951.

Maximilian I, The Triumph of, Woodcuts by Hans Burgkmair and others, Dover, New York, 1964.

Mersenne, Marin, *Harmonie Universelle*, Paris, 1636; reduced-size facsimile, CNRS, Paris, 1963.

Montagu, Jeremy, "The Construction of the Midwinterhoorn," *GSJ* XXVIII, 1975.

——, "The Eliphone—a 'Retreating Reed,'" *GSJ* LI, 1998.

——, "The Forked Shawm," *FoMRHIQ* 21, Comm. 304, October 1980.

——, "The Forked Shawm—an Ingenious Invention," *Yearbook for Traditional Music*, Vol.29, 1997.

——, *Reed Instruments*, Bate Collection, Oxford, 1986 *et seq.*

——, *The Scales of Music*, Bate Collection, Oxford, 1994.

——, "The Society's First Foreign Tour," *GSJ* XXI, 1968.

——, *The World of Baroque & Classical Musical Instruments*, David & Charles, Newton Abbot, 1979.

——, *The World of Medieval & Renaissance Musical Instruments*, David & Charles, Newton Abbot, 1976.

——, *The World of Romantic & Modern Musical Instruments*, David & Charles, Newton Abbot, 1981.

Montagu, Jeremy and John Burton, "A Proposed New Classification System," *Ethnomusicology* XV:1, 1971.

Moonen, Toon, "The Brussels Crumhorns: Hypotheses on their Historical Construction," *GSJ* XXXVI, 1983.

Morton, David, *The Traditional Music of Thailand*, University of California Press, Berkeley, 1976.

Moule, A. C., "A List of the Musical & Other Sound-Producing Instruments of the Chinese," *Journal of the Royal Asiatic Society, North China Branch*, NS 39, 1908.

Müller, Mette, "The Danish Skalmeje," *Studia instrumentorum musicae popularis* III, Musikhistoriska Museet, Stockholm, 1974.

Ord-Hume, Arthur W. J. G., *Harmonium*, David & Charles, Newton Abbot, 1986.

Picken, Laurence, *Folk Musical Instruments of Turkey*, Oxford University Press, 1975.

——, "Music of Far Eastern Asia" in Egon Wellesz (ed), *Ancient and Oriental Music—New Oxford History of Music* I, Oxford University Press, 1957.

——, "The Sound-Producing Instrumentarium of a Village in North-East Thailand," *Musica Asiatica* 4, Cambridge, 1984.

——, *et alii*, "The Making of a *khāēn*: The Free-Reed Mouth-Organ of North-East Thailand," *Musica Asiatica* 4, 1984.

Pierre, Constant, *Les Facteurs d'instruments de musique*, Sagot, Paris, 1893.

Rimmer, Joan, "The Instruments called Chirimia in Latin America," *Studia instrumentorum musicae popularis* IV, Musikhistoriska Museet, Stockholm, 1976.

Sa-Hun, Chang, *Korean Musical Instruments*, Seoul, 1969.

Sadie, Stanley (ed), *The New Grove Dictionary of Musical Instruments*, Macmillan, 1984.

Sárosi, Bálint, *Die Volksmusikinstrumente Ungarns; Handbuch der europäischen Volksmusikinstrumente I: Ungarns*, Deutsche Verlag für Musik, Leipzig, 1967.

Schlesinger, Kathleen, *The Greek Aulos*, Methuen, 1939.

Vertkov, K., G. Blagotatov, and E. Yazovitskaya, *Atlas of Musical Instruments of the Peoples Inhabiting the USSR*, State Music Publishers, Moscow, 1975.

Waterhouse, William, *The New Langwill Index*, Tony Bingham, 1993.

White, Paul, "Early Bassoon Reeds: A Survey of Some Important Examples," *JAMIS* X, 1984.

——, *The Early Bassoon Reed in relation to the Development of the Bassoon from 1636*, D.Phil. thesis, Oxford, 1993.

Williams, Peter, *A New History of the Organ*, Faber, 1980.

Young, Phillip T., *4900 Historical Woodwind Instruments*, Tony Bingham, 1993.

——, *Die Holzblasinstrumente im Oberösterreichischen Landesmuseum*, Linz, 1997.

Yupho, Dhanit, *Thai Musical Instruments*, Department of Fine Arts, Bangkok, 1960.

Indices

INDEX OF CATALOGUE NUMBERS

INDEX OF INSTRUMENT NAMES

INDEX OF MAKERS AND DEALERS

INDEX OF DONORS & VENDORS

GEOGRAPHICAL INDEX

GENERAL INDEX

This index should be used in conjunction with the Table of Contents and the special indices; so far as possible overlapping has been avoided.

ב"ה